Dear friends
We are not a glum lot,
if newcomers see no
joy in the way we live
they wont want it. So
we absolutely insist on
enjoying life. P. 132
Your friend
John Kerr

ALCOHOLICS ANONYMOUS
80 Years—Happy, Joyous and Free
2015 A.A. International Convention
Atlanta, Georgia / July 2-5, 2015

ALCOHOLICS ANONYMOUS

80 Years

HAPPY, JOYOUS *and* FREE

INTERNATIONAL A.A. CONVENTION
Atlanta, Georgia ✳ July 2-5, 2015

CONTENTS

A.A. PREAMBLE®

Alcoholics Anonymous is a fellowship of men and women who share their experience, strength and hope with each other that they may solve their common problem and help others to recover from alcoholism.

The only requirement for membership is a desire to stop drinking. There are no dues or fees for A.A. membership; we are self-supporting through our own contributions.

A.A. is not allied with any sect, denomination, politics, organization or institution; does not wish to engage in any controversy; neither endorses nor opposes any causes.

Our primary purpose is to stay sober and help other alcoholics to achieve sobriety.

WELCOME

With deep gratitude, we gather to celebrate 80 years of carrying the A.A. message of hope throughout the world. Today, happy, joyous and free, we celebrate Alcoholics Anonymous!

It is said that those most capable of gratitude are those who have emerged from the darkness of alcoholism into the light of sobriety. A.A. is a powerful Fellowship of light and gratitude because you have welcomed millions to walk with purpose on the road of recovery.

Our gratitude extends to Bill W. and Dr. Bob; to our early pioneers; to the millions of recovered alcoholics and friends of A.A. who have gone before; to the members of our worldwide Fellowship not able to be here; and to all who have traveled to this celebration. And we are grateful to a power greater than ourselves that inspires us in all our endeavors.

We also celebrate *Alcoholics Anonymous*, our Big Book. This text has helped save millions of lives from alcoholism and is recognized as one of the most influential books ever written, with over 40 million copies printed worldwide.

As we see the world shrink through the amazing advances in digital communication, let us employ these cutting edge methods to ensure that the hand of A.A. always will be there for anyone, anywhere on this small planet Earth, always keeping in mind the vitally important principle of anonymity in all our affairs.

Each of us involved with A.A. has an obligation to those not yet here—of keeping the doors of a meeting open to those who may need A.A. so desperately—no matter who they are or what their background is. We also have an obligation to the newcomer to make sure the message remains clear and strong.

May we truly be happy, joyous and free as we continue into our 9th decade of trudging the road of happy destiny together—one day at a time!

Terrance M. Bedient

Terrance M. Bedient, FACHE
Chairman, General Service Board of Alcoholics Anonymous

The Akron living room of Oxford Group members T. Henry and Clarace Williams, where A.A. Group Number One began.

PART ONE

The Early Years

BILL'S JOURNEY

"To my beloved wife that has endured so much, let this stand as evidence of my pledge to you that I have finished with drink forever." - OCTOBER 20, 1928

"[I] tell you once more that I am finished with it. I love you." - JANUARY 1929

"Finally and for a lifetime, thank God for your love." - SEPTEMBER 3, 1930

Bill Wilson

At the time he inscribed these promises to his wife Lois on the flyleaf of the family Bible, Bill Wilson was a rising star on booming 1920s Wall Street, living in a two-bedroom apartment in a fine residential neighborhood in Brooklyn, New York, dreaming of someday serving on the board of directors of a powerful financial company.

And yet, like thousands of alcoholics before and since, no matter how hard he tried, no matter what promises he made, Bill Wilson could not stop drinking. Once the closing bell rang on Wall Street, he would head immediately for a speakeasy. "I would start out with $500 and then have to crawl under a subway gate to get back to Brooklyn," he later wrote, a prodigious feat of carousing when you remember that $500 in 1928 money had the buying power of almost $7,000 today.

In the fall of 1933, Bill, despairing and unemployable, entered Charles B. Towns Hospital on Manhattan's West Side. Towns Hospital was essentially a drying-out facility, where drunks were given powerful laxatives and purgatives, as well as barbiturates to help them through withdrawal symptoms. But it was here that Bill, in the first of a series of encounters that would shape the future course of Alcoholics Anonymous, met Dr. William Duncan Silkworth.

A diminutive, white-haired man, Silkworth was ahead of his time in embracing the radical concept that alcoholism is just as much a disease as the common cold or cancer, and that willpower cannot overcome it. Bill enthusiastically accepted this, but a few short months after leaving Towns, he drank again. Despite three more stays at Towns over the course of the next twelve months, he was unable to stop bingeing. Even the sympathetic Silkworth confided to Lois that Bill's alcoholism was hopeless, progressive and irreversible, and that Bill might need to be confined.

In November 1934, however, a fellow Vermonter and old drinking buddy named Ebby T. visited Bill at his Brooklyn apartment. Ebby had gotten sober under the auspices of the Oxford Group, a nondenominational Christian move-

The flyleaf of the Wilson family Bible, where Bill made his fervent promises to Lois.

ment popular in the United States and Europe at the time. He convinced Bill to attend a few meetings. Bill felt himself drawn to the Oxford people he met, although he would come to resist what he later called the group's "very dynamic and sometimes very aggressive form of evangelism." Continuing to drink, he ended up in Towns again in December 1934, having just turned thirty-nine. He was sinking once again into what he termed "the terrifying darkness" of alcoholism and felt there was nowhere for him to turn. On the night of December 11, Bill surrendered and underwent what has been referred to as "a white light experience"—in effect, a spiritual awakening. Bill Wilson never drank again. But it was not in his nature to keep his extraordinary experience to himself.

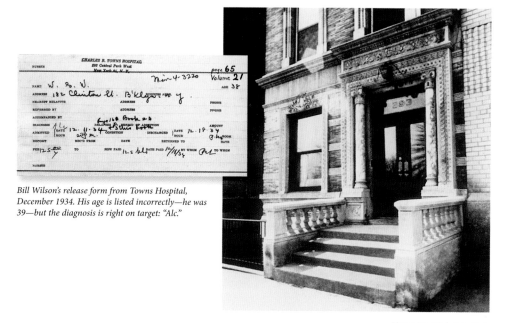

Bill Wilson's release form from Towns Hospital, December 1934. His age is listed incorrectly—he was 39—but the diagnosis is right on target: "Alc."

Towns Hospital, New York.

THE WASHINGTONIANS ～ Coming even before the Oxford Group, an early organization that sought to help alcoholics was the Washingtonian Society, formed in the 1840s. At its peak, the group may have had as many as 500,000 members. The Washingtonians paralleled A.A. in a number of ways. Only drunks could address the other drunks at early Washingtonian meetings; sharing personal stories became a way for members to identify and connect; and people professed a belief in a Higher Power. Unfortunately, the Washingtonian movement died out by 1850, due in large part to the fact that the group became politicized around the abolitionist and temperance movements. Bill W. studied this group closely, understanding, as he wrote, that they "lost their effectiveness" when they allied themselves with other causes.

"The Rum Hound From New York"

During the first months of 1935, Bill joined the Oxford Group, began to attend meetings, and attempted to bring other alcoholics to sobriety. He was disappointed that none remained sober for long. Dr. Silkworth identified the reason as Bill's preaching—about the Oxford Group and about his own visionary experience—and advised him to "get out of the driver's seat" and simply talk directly about his own experiences as a drunk and the fact of alcoholism as an illness.

In May, Bill made a visit to Akron, Ohio, in pursuit of a business deal that unfortunately soured. Left to face a lonely weekend before returning home, he found himself drawn more and more to sounds of a happy crowd drinking in the hotel bar, and realized that the only thing that would keep him sober was talking to another alcoholic. Spying a directory of churches and their ministers in the lobby, he picked a name at random—the Episcopalian minister William F. Tunks—and called him to seek help.

Tunks put Bill in touch with an Akron Oxford Group member named Henrietta Sieberling, who told him about a local doctor, Bob S., whose drinking caused him terrible anguish. She arranged a meeting between the two men on the evening of Sunday, May 12. Dr. Bob was fifteen years older than Bill (whom he considered "the rum hound from New York") and horribly hungover that evening, but the two men were fellow Vermonters and hit it off. They spoke for five hours. Bob would go on to drink again a few weeks later, but would stop for good on June 10, 1935, which is celebrated as the founding date of Alcoholics Anonymous.

Extending his stay in Akron, Bill moved in with Bob, his wife Anne, and their two children. During the course of long conversations, the two men realized that to stay sober they needed to find other alcoholics like themselves. They practiced what they might say to them, hitting upon one of the basic tenets of A.A.—the fact that it was far easier for drunks to think of stopping drinking for twenty-four hours, rather than a lifetime.

It was now merely a matter of finding another alcoholic in need of help. After failing to sober up a socially prominent alcoholic named Eddie R. (Eddie pulled a knife on Bill at one point), Bill and Bob soon found "A.A. Number 3" at Akron City Hospital in the form of a lawyer named Bill D., whose story in the first edition of the Big Book is entitled "The Unbeliever." After Bill D. came Ernie G., who would later relapse—his Big Book tale is entitled "The Seven Month Slip"—but when Bill caught a train to return to New York in late August, the program, still unnamed, was growing slowly.

Dr. Bob Smith

The home of Dr. Bob and Anne, 855 Ardmore Avenue, Akron.

BEGINNING TO SPREAD THE WORD

Back east, Bill sought prospects at Towns Hospital, where he helped sober up two early New York A.A.s, Hank P. and Fitz M., who became his close friends and allies. He set up a Tuesday night meeting at his home at 182 Clinton Street in Brooklyn. He also attended Oxford Group meetings at Calvary Church in Gramercy Park, bringing with him his group of struggling alcoholics, but gradually friction grew between the Oxford Group members who were not drunks and the new A.A.s. The Oxford Group did not like Bill holding separate meetings at Clinton Street, while the alcoholics felt that the nonalcoholics within the Oxford Group did not fully appreciate their problems.

While acknowledging the help he had received from the Oxford Group, Bill reluctantly left the group in 1937 (the Akron alcoholics and Dr. Bob would follow suit in 1939). One alcoholic, Jim B., described Clinton Street meetings around this time as having little in the way of "creed or procedure" to guide them, except for the Bible and a few leftover sayings from the Oxford Group. But A.A. as we know it today was gradually being formed. Charles Towns suggested that Bill move his work to Towns Hospital, where he could both reach alcoholics and share in the institution's profits. Bill, perpetually broke, thought this was a great idea—until he arrived at Clinton Street to find members of the meeting strongly against it, insisting that taking money would violate the integrity of the program. Thus was born the group conscience, as well as the idea that A.A. should never endorse any outside facility or program.

Late in 1937, two and a half years after he and Dr. Bob had met, Bill W. took a trip to Detroit and Cleveland in search of work. He did not find any, but stopped in Akron to see Bob and his family. One day, the two men decided to do a "formal" review of their efforts so far. By enumerating everyone whom they knew to be sober, in both New York and Akron, they realized that roughly forty alcoholics were not drinking because of the program they had developed. As Bill would later write:

"As we carefully rechecked this score, it suddenly burst upon us that a new light was shining into the dark world of the alcoholic . . . [A] benign chain reaction, one alcoholic carrying the good news to the next, had started outward from Dr. Bob and me. Conceivably it could one day circle the whole world. What a tremendous thing that realization was. At last we were sure. There would be no more flying totally blind."

"500 EX-SOUSEPOTS SNUB PINK ELEPHANT": A.A. AND THE PRESS ~ When knowledge of A.A. first began to trickle out to the public, the press handled it with some uneasiness. Headlines like "500 Ex-Sousepots Snub Pink Elephant" and "Bottle Babies No More" vied with more serious approaches such as "100 Alcoholics Lock Arms in Sobriety." While the concept of personal anonymity lies at the heart of A.A., Bill W. and other early members were hungry for publicity for the program itself, so that more and more alcoholics might find their way to sobriety. The first significant break came when Dr. Charles Towns, who had founded the hospital where Bill had had his spiritual awakening, convinced a reporter for *Liberty* magazine to write an article about A.A. Although Bill thought the title of the piece—"Alcoholics and God"—might scare off some alcoholics, the September 1939 article sold several hundred Big Books and brought in more than 800 inquiries from alcoholics and their loved ones. A month later, a five-part series on A.A. appeared in the *Cleveland Plain Dealer*, which brought in more inquiries and book orders. "A.A. was on the march out of its infancy and into its adolescence," Bill wrote.

But A.A. didn't reach full adulthood (press-wise) until the famous *Saturday Evening Post* article by Jack Alexander, published on March 1, 1941. The article, which portrayed A.A. members with empathy, gave hope to alcoholics and their families everywhere. Membership in A.A grew from 2,000 to 8,000 by the end of the year. Within a decade it had swollen to more than 96,000.

THE BIG BOOK

"We have concluded to publish an anonymous volume setting forth the problem as we see it. We shall bring to the task our experience and knowledge. This should suggest a useful program for anyone concerned with a drinking problem."

—THE BIG BOOK, CHAPTER TWO, PAGE 29

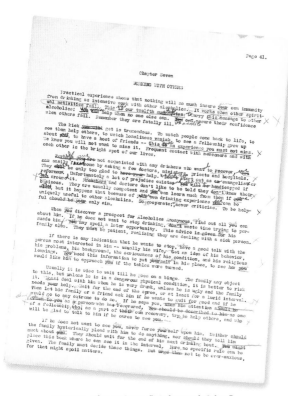

First page, Chapter Seven, "Working with Others"

While Bill and Dr. Bob were pleased to count forty sober alcoholics when they met that day in 1937, they also knew that there were millions of sufferers worldwide who desperately needed to find sobriety. How was the message to be brought to them?

Bill, the born-promoter, envisioned building missions and even establishing special hospitals for alcoholics alone. Bill also proposed a book that would explain the program to alcoholics and keep its message from being distorted. But Dr. Bob, while liking the idea of a book, was leery of paying people to carry the message.

To help settle the matter, the two men met with eighteen Akron alcoholics, who narrowly voted to approve the paid missionary scheme. Bill's group back in New York City was more enthusiastic, but only if Bill could raise the money necessary to launch this grand program. Bill tried his best. In the fall of 1937, he turned to his brother-in-law, Dr. Leonard Strong, who helped arrange a series of meetings with men connected to the philanthropies of John D. Rockefeller. In a meeting in December at Rockefeller Center, attended by Bill, Dr. Bob,

and others, it was decided that funding on a large scale would compromise the purpose and mission of the fledgling program. Out of this meeting, however, would came the creation of the Alcoholic Foundation (forerunner of the General Service Board), which was formally established in August 1938, and would handle any incoming funds and provide organizational structure for the group.

With immediate hopes of funding shot down, Bill turned to the one component of the plan which he could work on immediately: writing a book. Bill began working on what would become the Big Book in March or April 1938. His base of operations for writing it was the offices of Honor Dealers, a gasoline cooperative business he had set up with fellow alcoholic Hank P. at 17 William Street in Newark, NJ. As their nonalcoholic and often unpaid secretary, Ruth Hock, would later write, the business went nowhere, mainly because Bill and Hank were more interested in "helping a bunch of nameless drunks."

Bill's process in writing the Big Book was to arrive at the office with loose sheets of yellow paper that contained notes outlining each of the chapters. He would dictate to Ruth as she sat at her typewriter and then read over the typescript, making corrections. He would then have the chapters copied and sent out to Akron and Dr. Bob to be reviewed, while he himself would go over them with his group of New York alcoholics. (Bill would remember that he got "nothing but the warmest reception" from Akron, but "a real mauling" from New York.)

Most of the discussion centered on how much God was too much God—many members wanted the book more religious in nature, while others felt that a book too centered on a Christian God would put off those alcoholics who were atheist or agnostic.

When the book was at last done, late in January 1939, it contained eleven chapters and twenty-nine powerful personal stories that Bill described as "the written equivalent of hearing speakers at an A.A. meeting." The manuscript still lacked a title, however. Akron and New York members had had discussions on the matter, and the name *Alcoholics Anonymous*— probably already in use informally among New York members—was an early favorite. So, however, was *The Way Out*. It was not until an A.A. member visited the Library of Congress and discovered that there were twelve books entitled *The Way Out* already in existence—but none called *Alcoholics Anonymous*—that the group settled on the latter as its title. Thus A.A. got its name and its book. A first printing of 5,000 copies was published in April 1939. Most of these were to languish in a warehouse until A.A. began to receive publicity from various news outlets, most notably Jack Alexander's famous *Saturday Evening Post* article in 1941, but the Big Book became a huge success story. Its four editions, translated into 68 different languages and read by people in 170 different countries, have sold 35 million copies. It continues to sell at the rate of one million copies per year.

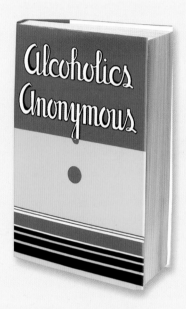

Nearly 80 years and four editions later, 35 million copies sold.

A Book Designed for Alcoholics

Ironically, despite the debate among early members over what to call the book, it would forever be known simply as the Big Book. This was because Bill decided to price the book at $3.50, rather steep for the spring of 1939. When the manuscript was delivered to the printer, Bill and Hank P. chose the thickest paper possible, in order, as Bill later wrote, "to convince the alcoholic purchaser that he was getting his money's worth." Ruth Hock, however, was under the impression that the Big Book's large size (and relatively large typeface) was intended for alcoholics who were too shaky to read fine print or turn thin pages.

THE TWELVE STEPS: "God As We Understood Him"

The process of writing the Big Book went relatively quickly through the first four chapters—"Bill's Story," "There Is A Solution," "More About Alcoholism," and "We Agnostics." But when Bill reached what would become Chapter Five—"How It Works"—he became stuck. Here was the moment when he needed to explain exactly how a despairing alcoholic would be able to find sobriety.

Bill had already come up with six steps loosely based on Oxford Group precepts, but he felt that they needed to be broken into "smaller pieces," both to make them more understandable and to deepen the spiritual implications of the program. One night, lying in bed at 182 Clinton Street with what he called "one of my imaginary ulcer attacks," he asked for guidance, picked up one of the cheap yellow-paper tablets

he used, and began writing. Suddenly, words tumbled out of him, and within half an hour, he had an outline of the Twelve Steps.

But when Bill showed the Steps to New York members for review, a heated debate ensued. It was the classic argument between those who wished the program to explicitly espouse Christian doctrine—Bill's draft talked a great deal about God and referenced asking "on one's knees" to have one's shortcomings removed—and those who thought this would be off-putting to nonbelievers. Finally, a brilliant compromise was struck. The phrase *"God as we understood him"* was added to the Third Step. Bill later called this "the great contribution of our atheists and agnostics. They had widened the gateway so that all who suffer might pass through. . . ."

The Principles Of "AA"

These are the 12 principles of "Alcoholics Anonymous:"

1. "We admitted we were powerless over alcohol—that our lives had become unmanageable.
2. "Came to believe that a Power greater than ourselves could restore us to sanity.
3. "Made a decision to turn our will and our lives over to the care of God as we understood Him.
4. "Made a searching and fearless moral inventory of ourselves.
5. "Admitted to God, to ourselves and to another human being the exact nature of our wrongs.
6. "Were entirely ready to have God remove all these defects of character.
7. "Humbly asked Him to remove our shortcomings.
8. "Made a list of all persons we had harmed, and became willing to make amends to them all.
9. "Made direct amends to such people wherever possible, except when to do so would injure them or others.
10. "Continued to take personal inventory and when we were wrong, promptly admitted it.
11. "Sought through prayer and meditation to improve our conscious contact with God as we understood Him, praying only for knowledge of His will for us and the power to carry that out.
12. "Having had a spiritual experience as the result of these steps, we tried to carry this message to alcoholics and practice these principles in all our affairs."

1942 newspaper article listing the "Principles" (Twelve Steps).

"DEFOGGING": THE EVOLUTION OF TWELFTH STEP WORK ∼ After Bill and Dr. Bob parted in 1935, each sought fellow alcoholics to bring into the A.A. fold. They generally found them in area hospitals—Bill in Towns Hospital in New York, and Bob at Akron City Hospital, Akron General Medical Center, and St. Thomas Hospital (with the aid of the indefatigable Sister Ignatia). There were some miscues—Bob was reluctant to give up a special diet he prescribed for newly sober alcoholics, which consisted of sauerkraut, tomatoes and Karo syrup—but the early A.A.s, especially in the Midwest, developed a fairly rigid Twelfth-stepping protocol. During this period, A.A. was not the program of attraction it became later (you had to be sponsored to walk into an Akron or Cleveland meeting). Instead, Dr. Bob or another A.A. would speak first with the man's wife (since those being Twelfth-stepped were almost always men) and ask her if her husband truly wanted to recover. After that, the alcoholic in question would generally be hospitalized in order to be "defogged," as it was called. When the fog had cleared, he would be visited every day by all the A.A.s in the town (in these early years, not too big a crowd) and finally brought to meetings.

SISTER IGNATIA AND A.A. ~ Sister Mary Ignatia, who worked in the admissions staff of St. Thomas Hospital in Akron, had met and liked Dr. Robert Smith long before he came to her one day in 1939 and confessed that he was an alcoholic. Not only that, he said, but he had teamed up with a "New York broker" he had come in contact with and was helping fellow alcoholics stay sober. Would Sister Ignatia consider admitting one of these alcoholics to St. Thomas?

With some trepidation, she said she would, and thus began her fabled career helping drunks, first at St. Thomas, and then in Cleveland, at St. Vincent Charity Hospital, where she was placed in charge of the alcoholic ward.

The following is an excerpt from a speech she gave before the Third International A.A. Convention in Long Beach, California, in 1960, describing her experiences with one of Dr. Bob's drunks and the "fine-looking men" who came to visit him.

"Dr. Bob said: 'Would you mind putting my patient in a private room? You know, there will be some men come to visit him and they like to talk to him privately.'

"After he left, I went up and looked the situation over, and right across the hall we had a flower room where we used to prepare the patients' flowers, and I thought, *well, they can fix their flowers somewhere else for today and I believe I can push the bed in there.* That's what we did. And his visitors came. We kept a close eye on them. I did! It was all new and I thought: *What mighty, respectable-looking men. They don't look like they ever took a drink.*

"[After a while] the [visitors] were coming in quite often. So much so that some of the Sisters said: 'Who are these fine-looking men? They come in so often and seem so interested in the patients?'

"I didn't say much at first, but later I said: 'Well, that is A.A.'

"'What is A.A.?'

"'Would you like to know something about it?'

"'Well, yes.'

"'Well, I'll bring you some literature then.'"

Dr. Bob and Sister Ignatia's close relationship would continue throughout the 1940s, as, together, they helped sober up literally thousands of drunks. A poignant postscript: In 1952, two years after Bob's death, Sister Ignatia was transferred to St. Vincent's in Cleveland. At her suggestions, the alcoholic ward was named the Rosary Hall Solarium, with the initials "R.H.S." carved over the door.

R.H.S., of course, just happened to be the initials of Dr. Robert Holbrook Smith.

GRAPEVINE: The International Journal of Alcoholics Anonymous

In the spring of 1944, six New York A.A. members decided to create a newsletter for area alcoholics. They took the idea to Bill W., who liked it enough to suggest that these "ink-stained wretches," as he called them, might like to expand it into a national magazine for A.A.s. The first issue of Grapevine appeared as an eight-page newspaper in 1944, costing fifteen cents. A free copy was sent to every A.A. group in the country—about 300—and to all known A.A. members spread around the world in the armed forces. Grapevine had a special section for service personnel, entitled "Mail Call For All A.A.s in the Armed Forces," which was devoted to letters from members who had nicknamed Grapevine their "meeting in print."

From the very beginning, the magazine has published first-person stories written by alcoholics describing their personal struggles, joys and sorrows. For a long time, however, Grapevine's most prolific contributor was Bill W. himself, who spoke of the magazine as "a mirror of the Fellowship" and "a forum for debate." Importantly, Bill would use Grapevine to set forth and elaborate on the Twelve Traditions; to provide glimpses into A.A. history, from the origin of the Twelve Steps to stories of Dr. Bob and Sister Ignatia; and to publish his exchange of letters with Dr. Carl Jung. The A.A. Preamble originally appeared in Grapevine in June 1947, written by the Grapevine's then-editor Tom Y. and drawing on the Foreword of the original edition of the Big Book. And

in an article published in the December 1950 issue of the magazine—just after Dr. Bob's death in November—Bill first suggested that he and Bob felt that the membership should take over the affairs of A.A. as a whole through the mechanism of a General Service Board.

AAGV, Inc. was incorporated as one of two service arms of the Alcoholic Foundation (now known as the General Service Board) in 1945. It changed from its newspaper format to the present-day digest size in 1948, but continues its original mission, more than 70 years later, to carry the A.A. message to alcoholics and to practice A.A. principles in all its affairs. AAGV, Inc. publishes a bimonthly Spanish-language magazine, *La Viña*, introduced in 1996, as well as invaluable Grapevine archives, featuring almost every story since 1944, available at www.aagrapevine.org. And Grapevine now publishes in print, audio, and digital formats online.

Grapevine, Vol. 1., No. I, June 1944.

2015 A.A. Grapevine and La Viña.

Aagrapevine.org. Home Page

La Viña

As the Spanish-speaking A.A. Fellowship in the U.S. and Canada grew phenomenally over the last several decades, Spanish-speaking A.A.s expressed a desire to read and submit articles to Grapevine in their own language. The 1991 General Service Conference recommended that Grapevine begin publishing at least one article in Spanish every month, which it did between 1991-1996.

The 1995 General Service Conference approved the publication of a bimonthly Spanish-language edition of Grapevine. The first issue of La Viña, featuring original Spnish-language stories, came off the presses in June 1996 and copies were distributed to subscribers in the United States, Canada, Mexico, Central and South America, the Caribbean and Europe. In addition to the print magazine, La Viña features service resources and a complimentary story for reading or listening on its dedicated web page at www.aagrapevine.org/espanol.

"Twelve Suggested Points": THE TRADITIONS

"I offer these suggestions," Bill W. wrote in the April 1946 edition of Grapevine, "neither as one man's dictum nor as a creed of any kind, but rather as a first attempt to portray that group ideal toward which we have assuredly been led by a Higher Power these ten years past."

"The suggestions" Bill spoke of were a draft of the Twelve Traditions contained in an article entitled "Twelve Suggested Points For A.A. Tradition." Alcoholics Anonymous had grown by leaps and bounds since Bill and Dr. Bob met in Akron, and Bill's farseeing concern was how to preserve the Fellowship's unity of purpose. During the 1940s, Bill read hundreds of letters from A.A. groups around the country describing the problems they faced—disputes at this early stage in A.A.'s growth revolved around group autonomy, singleness of purpose, endorsement of outside enterprises and the

like. The letter writers expected Bill to act as referee; things were made even more difficult by the fact that in many cases he was personally acquainted with the parties involved. (Occasionally, this could be an advantage, as when he told one complaining letter writer: "Come on, Chuck, let's try to wind up this nonsense. After all, this is Alcoholics Anonymous.")

It was out of this "welter of exciting and fearsome experience," as Bill put it, that the Twelve Traditions ("traditions," acknowledging that A.A. cannot have "rules") were born. The Traditions as put forth by Bill dealt with the basic purpose of A.A. groups—"to carry the message to the alcoholic who still suffers"— but also addressed issues of how A.A. groups should conduct themselves in their relationship with the outside world and with Alcoholics Anonymous itself.

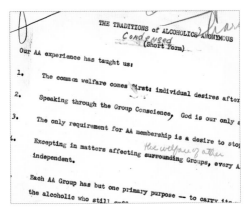

Early draft of the Twelve Traditions

After Bill's April 1946 Grapevine piece, the Twelve Traditions were published one by one in Grapevine, from December 1947 to November 1948, and adopted at the First International Convention in Cleveland in 1950. Each Tradition had been forged in the fire of a decade's hard experience—both Bill's and other A.A.s'— and each has stood the test of time.

BILL W., MAN OF LETTERS ∼ Despite his workload, Bill W. found the time to answer many of the thousands of letters that came across his desk. No question was too small. His April 1965 reply to Ford H. of Houston, Texas begins: "Thanks very much for your last letter in which you suggested a song for A.A.. It is rather odd, but nevertheless a fact, that never in the long history of A.A. has there ever been a move to adopt several proposed songs, nor a universal lapel button, nor a ring, or even a pocket token." When Mary H. of Grosse Ile, Michigan, expresses concern about swearing at meetings in 1966, Bill gently counsels her that a quiet suggestion to the offender is better than public castigation, adding: "I have, in earlier years, been reminded by friends that I shouldn't do this, either." (Invariably modest, Bill tells another correspondent: "Being just another rummy I keep on falling and stubbing my own toe anyhow.") Whether he's addressing the history of the use of the Lord's Prayer at the end of meetings (due to early influence of the Oxford Group) or cautioning an A.A. from Ann Arbor about writing a newspaper column that might break the anonymity of people in his home group, he often closes with the words: "My gratitude for your example of everything that is A.A."

Women Drunkards, Pitiful Creatures, Get Helping Hand

Regenerated Former Liquor Addicts, Members of Club "Alcoholics Anonymous," Tell of Their Fight for Sobriety

Carl Jung letter to Bill Wilson

A.A. #3: THE MAN ON THE BED ～ A stocky man with a charming drawl, Bill D. was a transplanted Kentuckian who practiced law in Akron and served on the city council. Despite his accomplishments, his alcoholism had landed him in the hospital eight times in the first half of 1935 alone, the last time with D.T.s so violent he had to be strapped to his bed. Undaunted, Bill, with seven months sobriety, and Bob, with only a few weeks, went to visit him in Akron City Hospital. Instead of "selling him religion," as Bill D. later put it, they told him of their own experiences and of their belief that alcoholism was a disease that could be arrested, one day at a time, with the help of other alcoholics. Bill D. left the hospital in July 1935 and never drank again. He's known in A.A. lore as "The Man on the Bed" because of a painting by the artist Robert M. that became a Grapevine center spread in 1955. Robert M. later presented the painting to Bill W., who hung it in his studio at Bedford Hills and wrote the artist: "The whole heart and essence of A.A. can be seen just by looking at it."

EARLY WOMEN IN A.A: ～ Born into a wealthy family, Marty M. was beautiful, intelligent and an alcoholic who lost job after job because of her drinking. After two suicide attempts, she was hospitalized at Blythewood Sanitarium, a private psychiatric center in Connecticut. A psychiatrist there gave her a copy of the mimeographed Big Book that was making the rounds in the spring of 1939. She read the book, at first with skepticism, but she gradually came to accept its message, and ended up attending the famous Tuesday night meeting at Bill and Lois's home at 182 Clinton Street in Brooklyn. The first bound copy of the Big Book was on display that night, and when Bill W. asked her to sign it, Marty realized she had found kindred spirits. She returned to Connecticut and said to a friend and fellow alcoholic: "Greenie, we are no longer alone."

Marty was the first woman in A.A. to achieve long-term sobriety, but she was followed by others: Florence R., Sylvia K., Ethel M., Sybil M. and Nona W. Not all stayed sober. As pioneers, they encountered difficulties: men were wary of women at meetings—Marty M. was told that women were "sneakier" than men, thus incapable of the honesty needed to stay sober. Even men who'd had terrible alcoholic bottoms considered women drunks "not nice." (This was made worse by the fact that nonalcoholic wives didn't want their husbands associating with women alcoholics.) Still, women persevered, and now they make up fully a third of A.A. membership.

"THE FIRST LINK": ROWLAND H., CARL JUNG AND THE PATH TO A.A. ～ In the early 1930s, a prominent American businessman journeyed to Zurich to visit the world-famous psychoanalyst Carl Jung. The man's name was Rowland H. and he was desperate to stop drinking. He spent about a year working with Jung, but when he left his care, he began drinking again. Even more desperate, Rowland returned, only to have Jung tell him bluntly that he suffered from an incurable condition that further psychoanalysis could not arrest. The only thing that might help Rowland now, Jung counseled, was a "spiritual awakening" in the form of a profound religious experience.

Shocked at this frank appraisal, Rowland soon joined the Oxford Group, where he had a conversion experience that lifted his compulsion to drink. Returning to America, he was instrumental in bringing Ebby T. to sobriety—and Ebby, in turn, helped sober up his friend Bill Wilson. Rowland H.'s conversation with Carl Jung would become a seminal moment in A.A. history. As Bill wrote in a grateful letter to Jung in 1961, it was "the first link in the chain of events that led to the founding of Alcoholics Anonymous."

COMMUNICATION, HISTORY, FELLOWSHIP:
The G.S.O. Newsletters

BOX 4-5-9 From the beginning of Alcoholics Anonymous, communication between A.A. Headquarters (now the General Service Office) and the growing number of A.A. groups across the country has been of paramount importance. One way of fostering this communication is G.S.O.'s quarterly newsletter, *Box 4-5-9*, with its articles on groups' collective problems and solutions, histories of the people and events that shaped A.A., and its invaluable Calendar of Events.

Box 4-5-9 first saw the light of day as *A.A. Bulletin*. The inaugural issue was written in November 1940 by Bill W.'s nonalcoholic secretary, Ruth Hock; its purpose, she said, was "an effort to develop a mutual idea exchange sheet between A.A. groups from the east coast to the west." In 1952, the name changed to the *Group Secretary*; in 1954 it became the *General Service Bulletin*; and in 1956 the name changed once again to the *A.A. Exchange Bulletin*. The *Exchange Bulletin* was longer (four pages) and was created "to fill many requests for a concise, movement-wide publication that would combine Headquarters news, basic information on A.A. as a whole, and brief accounts indicating how particular problems are being met by groups throughout the world."

The Holiday 1966 issue was the first to carry the name *Box 4-5-9* (the PO Box number of the General Service Office). For the first six years it was edited by Nell Wing, who had been for many years Bill W.'s secretary and had become A.A.'s first archivist; Nell considered it to be an invaluable "continuing picture" of A.A.'s growth and history. Currently 12 pages long and in four-color, *Box 4-5-9* is published in English, French and Spanish. To subscribe via email, go to www.aa.org and click on "G.S.O. Newsletters."

MARKINGS The idea of organizing an historical collection of A.A.'s records, manuscripts and artifacts began with Bill W. in the 1950s, but it took twenty more years before the General Service Office Archives formally opened its doors in November of 1975. Helping keep A.A. history alive, the G.S.O. newsletter *Markings: Your Archives eNewsletter* is published three times a year. *Markings* was first published in a print edition in February of 1981 and switched to an online-only format beginning in the summer of 2009.

Markings is a wonderful read for anyone interested in A.A. history. In it, area archivists exchange articles and photographs on group history. There's advice on how to preserve books and film collections for posterity. There are the stories of figures prominent in the history of A.A., from William James and Carl Jung to Nell Wing and Dr. Harry Tiebout. There are even articles about some of the minor (but enduring) mysteries of A.A., such as the exact date the Serenity Prayer was published in a New York newspaper. (It turned out to be May 28, 1941, in the Public Notices section of the *New York Herald-Tribune*.)

To subscribe to the *Markings* eNewsletter, in English, French or Spanish, go to www.aa.org and click on "G.S.O. Newsletters."

A.A. COMES OF (DIGITAL) AGE

http://www.aa.org

The August/September 1987 issue of *Box 4-5-9* carried an article entitled "A.A. Comes of (Computer) Age" in which an A.A. member describes their first A.A. meeting on an electronic bulletin board. "Any prospective user of such a bulletin board who has the requisite hardware (almost any computer), a modem, and the necessary communications software, may participate. First, he or she "logs-on," or initiates a connection to the board, and identifies him- or herself by handle (nickname). Thereafter, the user may read messages (sharings)."

The writer was generally pleased with the speed of connection ("like a meeting-by-mail…only infinitely faster") and speculated that "as more and more members become comfortable with PCs, heretofore unthought-of computer applications will evolve, as A.A Comes of (Computer) Age."

Although written nearly 30 years ago, this article was prescient; today, the digital age has revolutionized the way A.A.s connect with each other. Area and district websites provide meeting information. Private Facebook pages allow groups to connect online with anonymity. The Big Book and *Twelve Steps and Twelve Traditions* are available as ebooks; A.A.s can read them on their phones.

The official website of Alcoholics Anonymous, www.aa.org, was launched in 1995. It contains information on what to do if you are concerned about your drinking; contact information for local A.A. offices across the world;

digital copies of A.A. literature and pamphlets (including PDF versions of The Big Book and *Twelve Steps and Twelve Traditions*); A.A. history and archives; videos and audios; and a good deal more, available in English, French and Spanish. A.A. Grapevine also provides extensive online archives for its subscribers, as well as audio files in which A.A. members share their experience, strength and hope at www.aagrapevine.org.

THE DIGITAL AGE AND ANONYMITY

In a 1960 Grapevine article, Bill W. wrote: "Nothing matters more to A.A.'s future welfare than the manner in which we use the colossus of modern communication." He was speaking of television, radio, and print media, but the same statement can apply to the Internet. It is a tool through which A.A.s can connect and help each other stay sober, but it is also a tool to be used cautiously.

A.A.'s Internet guidelines suggest that A.A.s follow the Eleventh Tradition and not disclose A.A. membership on any social networking site (or blog, website or electronic bulletin board) that is not composed solely of A.A. members. This would include "status updates" in which sober anniversaries are disclosed. When setting up websites for local groups or service organizations, Alcoholics Anonymous trademarks and service marks—like "A.A.," "Alcoholics

Anonymous," and/or "The Big Book," should be avoided. (Use of lower case "aa" in website names is a good solution.)

Email is a great communication device, but needs to be treated with caution as well, since it is so easy to forward and cut and paste. In a group email, the email addresses of other A.A.s should be blind cc'd in order to preserve their anonymity, and last names should not be revealed.

Finally, when taking pictures of your A.A. friends at the Convention, think twice before you send the photos off with your smart phone to your favorite social media site or tweet them back home. Remember, anonymity is the spiritual foundation of the program, even (or especially) in the digital age.

A.A. IN POPULAR CULTURE

In the late 1930s and early 1940s, articles in *The Cleveland Plain Dealer*, *Liberty* magazine, the *Saturday Evening Post* and other publications brought in a flood of new members. Bill W. recounted how in A.A. offices, the phone would ring with queries that began: "I read a piece in the newspaper....We heard a radio program.... We saw a moving picture." The balance Bill, Dr. Bob, and other early A.A. members sought between "attraction" and "promotion" was never easily achieved, which is why the Eleventh Tradition developed as a guideline in the area of personal anonymity in the face of media attention.

And there was a lot of attention. American popular culture was quickly drawn to the story of A.A., which, with its undertones of tragedy and potential redemption, was rich with dramatic possibility. In the next decades, radio and television programs, movies, plays, comic strips and books poured forth, featuring struggling alcoholics attempting (not always with success) to make a go of it in A.A. Perhaps the most famous of these was the movie *The Lost Weekend*, based on the novel by Charles Jackson about a would-be writer lost in drink. Starring Ray Milland, it premiered in 1945, winning four Oscars. Afterward, three movie studios offered A.A. as much as $100,000 for the rights to the Fellowship's story, but the Alcoholic Foundation (forerunner of the General Service Board) refused.

While Alcoholics Anonymous could not lend its name to any commercial film, A.A.s themselves were not immune to the allure of the movies. An article in the January 1963 *A.A. Exchange Bulletin* (forerunner of *Box 4-5-9*) describes the staff of G.S.O. watching a screening of the movie *Days of Wine and Roses*—a powerful drama about an alcoholic married couple seeking help through A.A.—before it opened at Radio City Music Hall. They proclaimed it "marvelous."

L: *Oscar-winning fiim* The Lost Weekend
R: *Film poster for* Days of Wine and Roses.

A.A. IN THE MOVIES ～ Aside from *The Lost Weekend* and *Days of Wine and Roses*, portraits of alcoholics seeking to find their way into sobriety have appeared in numerous American films. Among them are:

MY NAME IS BILL W.: In an Emmy-winning performance, James Woods gives a moving portrayal of Bill Wilson.

BILL W.: Another Bill movie, only this time a documentary about his life.

WHEN A MAN LOVES A WOMAN: Starring Meg Ryan and Andy Garcia, this is the story of a "perfect" marriage threatened by a wife's alcoholism and her husband's reaction to it.

28 DAYS: Sandra Bullock stars as a party girl who is forced to get serious about her recovery at a rehab.

Above: Sobriety in the comics: "Wash Tubs" and A.A.'s own strips, "What Happened to Joe?" and "It Happened to Alice."
Top right: The Lasker Award.

THE LASKER AWARD ～ An important sign of recognition for Alcoholics Anonymous occurred in San Francisco in October 1951, when the American Public Health Association presented A.A. with the Lasker Award "in recognition of its unique and highly successful approach" to "an age-old public health and social problem." A ceremony on the previous evening, with Bill W. and the General Service Board chairman Bernard Smith, was attended by 3,000 A.A.s, family members, physicians, clergy, and public health experts.

"WASH TUBS" ～ In 36 panels running from April 4 to May 4, 1949, the renowned comic strip artist Leslie Turner told the story of alcoholic Gig Wilty, who is seeking help via A.A. The picture drawn of Wilty and his distraught friends and family is revealing and authentic and may be the first major portrayal of A.A. in a comic strip.

JOE AND ALICE GET SOBER ～ A.A.'s own comic strips, "What Happened to Joe?" and "It Happened to Alice," poignantly evoke the separate stories of a man and a woman who nearly lose everything before finding their way to the program.

AMERICAN WRITERS AND A.A. ～ The 20th century was a time when hard-drinking American writers were the norm rather than the exception. Nobelists like Sinclair Lewis, Eugene O'Neil, John Steinbeck, Ernest Hemingway, and William Faulkner were all heavy drinkers. None of these wrote about Alcoholics Anonymous. (F. Scott Fitzgerald, not a Nobelist, did mention A.A. once. "A.A. can only help weak people because their ego is strengthened by the group," said Fitzgerald. "I was never a joiner.")

Here are three notable books in which A.A. figures prominently:

One is Charles Jackson's *The Lost Weekend*. While the movie is far better known than the book, the latter is a superb and harrowing portrayal of Don Birnam, a would-be writer for whom "one drink was too many and a hundred not enough." Blake Bailey, Jackson's biographer, wrote that the novel "terrorized several early readers, all of them writers and heavy drinkers" since it hit so close to home. Jackson was sober when he wrote the book; unfortunately, he did not stay that way.

A classic memoir of A.A., writing and alcoholism is Donald Newlove's *Those Drinking Days: Myself and Other Writers*. Newlove describes his own journey to sobriety through broken marriages, automobile accidents, books that never got written, and desperate maintenance drinking. It's like a qualification in print: "First you hang on to all your old romances about your illness, then you suck your old grandiosity for every drop that's still in it…"

Finally, there is the late Carolyn Knapp's poignant *Drinking: A Love Story*. Published in the mid-1990s, it is an unstinting portrait of a woman who used alcohol as "liquid armor." Knapp loved everything about drinking and was proud of the fact that she could work as a journalist and editor and hold her own with men in her profession. But gradually her love affair with booze turned more and more destructive; she lied, cheated, and broke promises to those closest to her (including her dying parents). Finally, Knapp was able to enter rehab, attend regular A.A. meetings, and remained sober until her death in 2002.

Delegates voting at the April 1956 General Service Conference.

PART TWO

The Legacy of Service

THE GROUP

"The groups will eventually take over, and maybe they will squander their inheritance when they get it. It is probable, however, that they won't. Anyway, they really have grown up; A.A. is theirs; let's give it to them."

In the fall of 1937, having broken away from the Oxford Group, Bill W. held the first "completely alcoholic" meetings at his home at 182 Clinton Street in Brooklyn. According to Jim B., the gadfly agnostic who joined the group in January of 1938, "there were seven or eight men sitting around in a circle, with Bill W. in the center on a little three-legged stool, one of these old antique sewing stools. And he would do all the talking and we would do all the listening and answering the questions because he had all the book sense."

The early homes of A.A. in the East and Midwest
L. 182 Clinton Street, Brooklyn, N.Y.   R. The Williamses, Akron, Ohio

Even before the New York meetings, Akron alcoholics had begun to come together. In the summer of 1935, Bill W., Dr. Bob, Bill D.—A.A. Number Three, who Bill and Dr. Bob had helped sober up at Akron City Hospital—began to meet every Wednesday night at the home of T. Henry Williams and his wife Clarace, both nonalcoholic Oxford Group members. Ernie G., A.A. Number Four (who would marry Dr. Bob's daughter Sue), and Phil S., A.A. Number 5, were there, as well as Henrietta Seiberling and Anne Smith, Dr. Bob's wife. This was still an Oxford Group meeting; however, it had a solid nucleus of early A.A.s—"the alcoholic squad," they called themselves.

In these earliest days before the Big Book and the Twelve Steps, A.A.s read books like *The Sermon on the Mount* by Emmet Fox (which Dr. Bob made a point of giving to every potential A.A. he met in the hospital); *I Will Lift Up Mine Eyes* by Glenn Clark; and *The Greatest Thing in the World* by Henry Drummond, literature with a nondenominational spiritual or inspirational flavor. A hallmark of the early meetings at the Williamses' house, however, was taking new A.A. members to an upstairs room where they got on their knees and surrendered, admitting both their powerlessness over alcohol and the existence of a Higher Power who would return them to sanity. It was serious business. Ernie G. later recalled: "If by chance you didn't [make your surrender] at the hospital, you had to make it in the upstairs bedroom of the Williamses' house."

The meeting at the Williamses' moved to the King School in Akron in January of 1940. By this time, Clarence S., who had been sobered up by Dr. Bob, had founded the first A.A. group in Cleveland (probably, although not certainly, the first group to refer to itself as Alcoholics Anonymous). Clarence smuggled a *Cleveland Plain Dealer* reporter into a closed A.A. meeting; the resulting series of articles caused A.A. in Cleveland to spread faster than it had in either Akron or New York. As the Big Book was published and A.A. received publicity in magazines like the *Saturday Evening Post*, A.A. moved across the country, city by city, often carried by men newly sober, restored to jobs, and traveling on business.

At an A.A. meeting in Dayton in 1942, some members decided to wear masks when a newspaper reporter was present.

ANONYMITY AND PUBLIC INFORMATION ∿ By his own estimate, Bill W. turned down six honorary degrees from various universities, including one from Yale. He refused *Time* magazine's offer to place his picture on the cover (even if it was only the back of his head), despite the fact that, as he admitted, "a piece of this sort could have brought A.A. a thousand members—possibly a lot more."

Why is anonymity so important? On a basic level, it protects newcomers who may potentially be stigmatized in the eyes of some because of their disease. But anonymity is also about humility. As Tradition Twelve states: "Anonymity is the spiritual foundation of all our Traditions, ever reminding us to place principles before personalities." Bill W. admitted that his drinking career had centered around "an implacable pursuit of money, fame, and power" and that "tens of thousands of my fellow A.A.s are temperamentally just like me." To be humble, to work as part of Alcoholics Anonymous as a whole, can be difficult for A.A.s, but can also be the path to true spiritual growth.

However, providing information about A.A. to the public and the media is an important service task. Class A (nonalcoholic trustees) can act as the public face of the Fellowship, while Public Information Committees (the first Public Information Committee of the General Service Board was formed in 1956) make themselves available to speak in community settings—such as at schools, churches and health fairs—and cooperate with the media to provide information about upcoming A.A. Conventions or Regional Forums, etc.

By action of the General Service Board in January 1970, the trustees' Committee on Cooperation With the Professional Community (C.P.C.)—a spinoff from the Public Information Committee—was developed, and A.A. groups locally have created their own C.P.C. committees. C.P.C. committees reach out to health care professionals, clergy, legal professionals, social workers, and government officials with information about where to find A.A., what A.A. is, and what it can and cannot do.

But all of this crucial service contact with the community is done under the mantle of anonymity. As Bill W. reiterated in his "last message" to the Fellowship in October of 1970: "I deeply believe that the principle of anonymity must remain our primary and enduring safeguard. As long as we accept our sobriety in our traditional spirit of anonymity we will continue to receive God's grace."

THE BEGINNING OF INTERGROUPS ~ Established and supported by local groups to carry out the functions of a centralized office, intergroups have provided thousands of desperate alcoholics with their first contact with Alcoholics Anonymous, either online or over the phone.

In the early days, however, A.A. wasn't that easy to find. The phone numbers of members were given out only to a careful selection of priests, judges, and cops, in a deliberate effort to ensure that anyone wanting to get sober was sincere enough to make a real effort.

The true forerunner of today's Intergroup was a service center in the Chicago suburb of Evanston. Around 1940, an A.A. member named Sylvia used part of the proceeds of her monthly alimony check to rent an apartment and establish a phone line. With the aid of Grace Cultice, a nonalcoholic secretary, Sylvia's apartment became what Bill W. called "a sort of Chicago Grand Central," the phone constantly ringing off the hook. (Eventually, Sylvia and Grace had to upgrade to an office in the Loop.) Most early Intergroup offices were not even as elaborate as this—simply phone lines, listed as belonging to A.A., that plugged into members' homes. From Sylvia's alimony check arose numerous early Intergroup offices all over the Midwest, particularly ones in Green Bay, Wisconsin, and Minneapolis.

Going to any lengths....

TREATMENT FACILITIES: A.A.'S LONGEST SERVICE CONNECTION ~ Beginning back in 1935, when Bill W. and Dr. Bob visited Bill D., A.A. Number Three, in Akron City Hospital, A.A. has had a long association with treatment facilities. It is a natural connection, since when A.A. got started, hospitals where alcoholics were brought to dry out were places A.A.s gravitated to for Twelfth Step work. Dr. Bob's work with Sister Ignatia at St. Thomas Hospital reached more than 5,000 alcoholics, and Bill and Hank P. helped sober up alcoholics at Towns Hospital in New York.

In the earlier days, some A.A.s worked out private deals with hospitals to get them to admit alcoholics they had Twelfth-stepped. An example was Chicago's Washingtonian Home, a 1950s-era treatment center where A.A.-sponsored alcoholics were charged half the price of patients who entered without sponsorship and were kept segregated from non-A.A. patients under the theory that the latter simply wanted to dry out, not get sober.

Today, alcoholics on Treatment Facilities Committees go into institutions with the Sixth Tradition in mind: "An A.A. group ought never to endorse, finance, or lend the A.A. name to any related facility or outside enterprise, lest problems of money, property and prestige divert us from our primary purpose." Thus, an A.A. meeting in a treatment facility should never bear the name of that facility, although A.A.s may be asked to chair and run the meeting. A.A.s are there to explain how the program works to clients or staff; to give out literature; and to express their own experience, strength and hope.

Most importantly, A.A.s establish a presence to bridge the gap to the outside world, helping newly sober men and women make the tricky transition from the relatively sheltered environment of the treatment facility to their first A.A. meeting in the outside world.

St. Thomas Hospital, Akron.

A STRUCTURE ARISES

Gradually, A.A. began to evolve. The practice of introducing oneself as an alcoholic probably originated at some of the larger Oxford Group meetings, to differentiate alcoholics from non-alcoholics, although in Akron Prohibition-era terms like "drunk," "rum hound" or "boozer" were the preferred choice.

The idea of giving out chips or tokens to mark sober anniversaries probably began in Indianapolis in 1942, with Doherty S., who introduced A.A. to the city. Slogans like "Easy Does It," "First Things First," and "Live and Let Live" most likely arose from the Oxford Group by way of Bill W.

Since private homes soon became impractical for hosting large groups, A.A.s moved into various hotels, halls and churches, where rent had to be paid. Refreshments, too, had been a part of A.A. since the first Akron meeting moved to the King School (especially donuts from Kistler's, a local establishment); hence, the beginning of the Seventh Tradition of passing around the hat.

All of this meant that groups needed a functioning service structure—treasurers, chairpeople, secretaries, coffee-makers. Active alcoholics were not always welcomed—Clarence S. pointed out in 1940 that "several groups do not permit a rummy to attend unless he has been hospitalized or talked to by ten men"—but as the program grew and more and more people pleaded for help, alcoholics with only a few days sober might find themselves

L: King School, Akron. R: 24th Street Clubhouse, New York.

sponsoring a person drying out in a hospital. (To fulfill the same need, A.A. in New York established "under-six-months" meetings—the forerunner of today's beginners meetings—at the 24th Street Clubhouse, where New York A.A. had moved after Bill and Lois left their Clinton Street home in 1940.) Other sober alcoholics went into hospitals, treatment centers and prisons—one of the first prison A.A. meetings was held in San Quentin in 1942.

The first groups in A.A. were overwhelmingly white and male, but that slowly began to change. One of the first all-women's groups in A.A. started in Cleveland in June of 1941. Women in New York, Minneapolis, Salt Lake City and San Diego followed suit. Early in 1945, five African-Americans started a group in St. Louis; other all-black groups sprang up in Washington D.C., Los Angeles, New York, and New Jersey.

Bill and Lois took a cross-country journey in 1943–1944 to visit A.A. groups in Chicago, Denver, Los Angeles, San Francisco, Portland, Seattle, San Diego, Little Rock and Oklahoma City. In Little Rock, 1,200 people assembled for a meeting (the group leader spoke from behind a curtain, to preserve his anonymity). It was, in a certain sense, an introduction to A.A. for Bill. He and Dr. Bob had started the program, but now it had taken on a life of its own. In 1938, A.A. had barely 100 members. By 1946 there were 30,000 and by 1951 there would be 100,000. While this was cause for celebration, from Bill's point of view, it was also cause for concern.

A.A. IN CORRECTIONAL INSTITUTIONS: "Here was something real"

To be an active alcoholic in the American prison system, pre-Alcoholics Anonymous, was to be left to sort things out for yourself. Typically, an inmate might awaken in jail, having been arrested for a crime often committed during a blackout. "Treatment" would consist of enforced drying out, often combined with the D.T.s. Once a part of the main prison population, an alcoholic prisoner had the choice of white-knuckling it to stay sober or drinking homemade prison booze. After release, the chance that an ex-inmate would drink again—and commit more crimes—was high.

Only seven months after the first meeting in Philadelphia in 1940, A.A.s there visited the local jail. In fact, there were A.A. meetings in jails and prisons before some major towns had them. One of the first major prison groups was started in 1942 in California's San Quentin Prison with help from the famous warden Clinton T. Duffy. After this, A.A. spread to Folsom Prison, near Sacramento, started by the inmates themselves who decided, as one put it, "that here was something real." A.A. members from Sacramento devised an eight-week "instruction period," that included attending meetings on Sundays as well as a "graduation" on the eighth Sunday. (Although, as one A.A. wrote, prisoners "were given to understand that a man NEVER 'graduates' from A.A.")

A.A. Headquarters and Bill W. took note. Bill visited both Folsom and San Quentin in late 1943, finding 400 A.A.s in total at both prisons; when he returned east, he spoke at the Clinton Farms Reformatory for Girls in New Jersey. By 1945, there were A.A. groups in prisons in twelve states. Prison officials—including pioneering wardens like Duffy, Lee Henslee of Arkansas, Gus Harrison of Michigan and Alfred Dowd of Indiana—began to notice the low recidivist rate of A.A. members released on parole. By the 1950s, A.A. meetings had sprung up in prisons in other parts of the world, including Finland, Ireland, and Australia.

So many alcoholics in prison wrote to G.S.O. seeking help that by 1957, a staff member was devoted full-time to answering letters seeking correspondence; beginning in 1971, the G.S.O.'s Corrections Correspondence Service (CCS) provided inmates with "sponsorship via correspondence," connecting prisoners with outside A.A. members.

Currently, there are more than 1,500 A.A. groups in correctional facilities in the U.S. and Canada where inmates stay sober, one day at a time, like A.A.s everywhere.

SHARING FROM BEHIND THE WALLS: Prisoner Voices ~ The newsletter Sharing From Behind the Walls, published quarterly in English, French and Spanish by the Corrections assignment at G.S.O., is widely distributed to A.A.s in prison. It contains excerpts from inmate letters to G.S.O., published with permission, that capture the voices of A.A.s behind prison walls.

"My name is Jay, and I've used alcohol and drugs for 30 years. I am 45 now and have decided to quit drinking altogether. I have decided that alcohol is the root of my many arrests—17 due to my addictive lifestyle."—Jay M., East Central Region

"I am currently attending A.A. here every Tuesday and I'm grateful for the A.A. volunteers. Today I'm sober, although I still get that craving for a drink. I'm thankful to be alive and have another day sober, which isn't always easy."—Cynthia R., Pacific Region

"I am so happy to inform you that I am at last under six months prior to my release date…It seemed like this time would never come. Now that it has, could you please try to arrange a contact person for me in my hometown?…My new life begins in less than six months. I'm jittery, but more than ready."—Christian S., Southeast Region

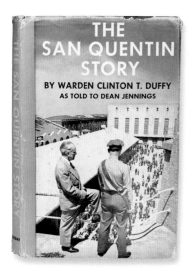

Warden Clinton T. Duffy wrote a book about his San Quentin reforms.

Early A.A. inmates published their own magazines.

CLINTON T. DUFFY: "I watched the inmates and visitors shaking hands..." ∼ The growth of A.A. within the prison system owes a great deal to the pioneering warden of California's San Quentin State Prison, Clinton T. Duffy. The son of a San Quentin prison guard, Duffy worked his way up from clerk to warden of the prison in 1940. At that time, prisoners were treated with brutality, and San Quentin had undergone uprisings, full-scale riots, and hunger strikes. Duffy instituted numerous humanitarian reforms, but was concerned about the fate of the alcoholic behind bars, particularly those who had committed crimes while under the influence. None of the social programs he instituted seemed to quite help these men, and his efforts at rehabilitation would be useless if they continued to drink. In his book *The San Quentin Story*, Duffy wrote: "The Alcoholics Anonymous movement was in its infancy then, but I communicated with some of the organizers in San Francisco and they agreed to come to San Quentin."

Under Duffy's auspices, an A.A. meeting was held at San Quentin in 1942. Twenty inmates attended, drawn by an announcement Duffy had placed in an inmate newspaper, the *San Quentin News*. Early inmates joining A.A. were dubbed "winos" by their fellow prisoners and met with skepticism by others who felt they could not possibly stay sober. But Duffy was to write that "A.A. men on parole have a consistently better record than other parolees." When he spoke at the First International Convention in Cleveland in 1950, Duffy talked about the close relationships formed between prisoners and visiting A.A.s. "When the meeting was over, and as I watched the inmates and visitors shaking hands, I knew that warm friendship and a feeling of mutual understanding had replaced the curiosity each group had felt for the other upon mutual introduction."

CORRECTIONS CORRESPONDENCE SERVICE: Lifeline by Letter ∼ Almost from the very first A.A. meeting behind bars, inmates wrote to A.A.s in the outside world and A.A.s responded. After Bill W.'s visit to San Quentin in late 1943, a prisoner named Clinton H. wrote: "I want to tell you how fortunate I was to have been present when you made your unforgettable visit...That was my first A.A. meeting—I haven't missed a meeting since."

Other inmate letters followed. A prisoner named Ken F., in the Philadelphia County Prison, wrote Bill in 1949 to praise his sponsor, an A.A. from outside the walls who "came to me and offered his hand that I be helped..." In 1957, Bill noted that one G.S.O. staff member "devotes her entire time almost exclusively" to inmate correspondence.

The 1971 General Service Conference recognized the importance of these letters between inmates and A.A.s in the outside world by supporting the efforts of the General Service Office to establish "an Institutions Correspondence Service on an individual basis, similar to the Loner-Sponsor Service." The G.S.O. staff member on the Corrections assignment receives approximately 35 letters a day from inmates who ask for literature or interim sponsorship. The Corrections Correspondence Service (CCS) connects an inmate with an outside A.A. member, so that they can share their experience, strength and hope.

Currently, several thousand A.A.s write to inmates, having received their addresses from G.S.O. Any A.A. member who would like to carry the message in this way can download a sign-up sheet from www.aa.org. As one inmate recently wrote: "The prison correspondence service (CCS) has made a big difference in my life. God has a wonderful way of working through people."

REMOTE COMMUNITIES: "I Am Responsible" ∽ Alcoholism is by its nature a disease that isolates and separates. When you add to that the separation experienced by alcoholics in far-flung communities—as well as alcoholics separated by language, culture or poverty from the mainstream—then getting sober can be even more difficult.

The idea of a Remote Community Meeting was conceived at the 50th Anniversary of A.A. in Montreal in 1985, when delegates met to discuss the problem of carrying the message to remote Canadian communities. There is now a Remote Communities Service Committee that reports at every General Service Conference. Solutions are sought to the problems of carrying the message to areas that are, as one Canadian alcoholic described, "a 20 hour car ride followed by a two hour plane ride and an hour by dog sled" away. Nor is it just Canada—Area 2 in Alaska averages 1.2 persons per square mile, with many communities accessible only by air. Other areas in the United States have Mennonite or Hispanic communities with language and cultural barriers, where children often have to interpret for parents entering the Fellowship.

Sometimes it's a matter of getting literature out to people in their native languages—translations of the Serenity Prayer, the Steps and the Traditions. At other times, the development of webinar series and videoconferencing can overcome barriers of distance, as well as the problems that may arise with anonymity when alcoholics reside in remote, close-knit communities. However they attempt to do it, A.A.s seeking to help alcoholics in remote communities epitomize the Responsibility Declaration: "When anyone, anywhere, reaches out for help, I want the hand of A.A. always to be there. And for that: I am responsible."

THE FIRST GENERAL SERVICE CONFERENCE

In the late 1940s, Bill came to believe that the survival of A.A. depended on involving groups more directly with the Alcoholic Foundation, formally implemented in 1938 to guide the affairs of A.A. The Foundation had fifteen (eight nonalcoholic and seven alcoholic) trustees, but little connection to A.A. groups except through Bill W. and Dr. Bob (who was now ill with the cancer that would take his life in 1950). In order to close what he called "this gap of remoteness," Bill proposed that groups elect regional representatives to attend a yearly "General Service Conference of Alcoholics Anonymous" to discuss issues of importance to A.A. with the trustees, the staff of the A.A. Headquarters office and Grapevine, and then make a "joint annual report to the Groups."

Predictably, most of the trustees were against such a plan; they feared that a crowd of alcoholics gathering from the hinterlands would interfere with what one trustee wrote Bill was the "degree of isolation [needed] in dealing with the necessary 'housekeeping,' legal, and financial affairs of the A.A. headquarters." At first reluctant, Dr. Bob gave his blessing to the plan and, with the help of nonalcoholic trustee Bernard Smith, the first General Service Conference was finally held in New York over three days in April 1951, with thirty-seven delegates from the United States and Canada. What Bill called the "politics and uproar" of whether to hold the Conferences (three trustees had resigned over the issue) was worth it. After

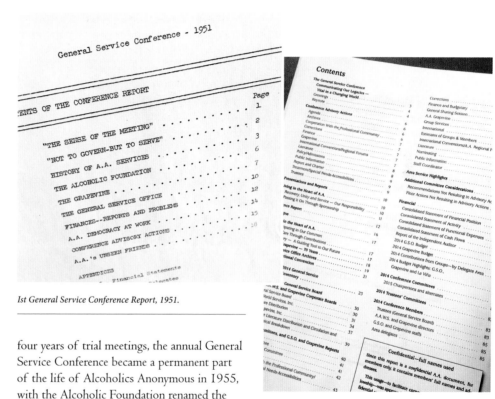

Ist General Service Conference Report, 1951.

64th General Service Conference Report, 2014.

four years of trial meetings, the annual General Service Conference became a permanent part of the life of Alcoholics Anonymous in 1955, with the Alcoholic Foundation renamed the General Service Board.

SERVICE FROM THE HOME GROUP OUTWARD

Alcoholics Anonymous now has more than 115,000 groups worldwide; these groups hold what Bill W. called "the ultimate responsibility and final authority for our world services." Bill's vision, further explained in his *Twelve Concepts for World Service* adopted by the General Service Conference in 1962, has provided a lasting service structure for the Fellowship. Importantly, Concept Twelve lists the General Warranties drawn up for the Conference Charter, which are worth repeating in their entirety:

General Warranties of the Conference:

In all its proceedings, the General Service Conference shall observe the spirit of the A.A. Tradition, taking great care that the conference never becomes the seat of perilous wealth or power; that sufficient operating funds, plus an ample reserve, be its prudent financial principle; that none of the Conference Members shall ever be placed in a position of unqualified authority over any of the others; that all important decisions be reached by discussion, vote, and whenever possible, by substantial unanimity; that no Conference action ever be personally punitive or an incitement to public controversy; that though the Conference may act for the service of Alcoholics Anonymous, it shall never perform any acts of government; and that, like the Society of Alcoholics Anonymous which it serves, the Conference itself will always remain democratic in thought and action.

The entire structure of A.A. starts with the home group, and it is at the home group that an A.A. member is most likely to do service—everything from tasks like stacking chairs or making coffee to chairing a meeting or becoming a district representative. The home group anchors an A.A. member in the program; taking a service commitment often means showing up because you don't want to let the group down.

Today, there is enormous variety in A.A. groups. There are beginners meetings, Big Book meetings, Step meetings, Tradition meetings and meditation meetings. Because each group is autonomous, meeting formats vary.

In Michigan, alcoholics gather at tables, each a meeting in itself; in Delaware, people stand to share Quaker-style, as the spirit moves them; on the East Coast, speaker-discussion meetings are common. Some meetings close with the Serenity Prayer; others with the Lord's Prayer. Meetings take place in the heart of busy cities and in the earth's remotest communities. And yet each home group, its direction determined by group consciences, makes decisions that reverberate outward to the general service level. The old joke is that all it takes to start an A.A. meeting is a coffee pot and a resentment; there may be a kernel of truth in that, but the greater truth is that A.A.s all over the world have found through service a unique way of staying sober and helping others to achieve sobriety.

1930s coffeepot from the South Orange (New Jersey) Group.

MEMBERSHIP

THE SLIP SQUAD ∿ In 1943, the A.A. Headquarters in New York asked groups to send in their membership rules. They were a trifle shocked by the number and variety they received.

For instance, the Wilson Club, which was a meeting space for A.A. groups in St. Louis around 1942, was very specific about slips. As it informed its members: "The Wilson Club does not condone 'slipping' nor does it welcome habitual slippers and 'back-door' A.A.s to its membership." After a first slip, a member would be compelled to "admit his drunkenness to the group." After a second, he or she would be forced to "turn in his membership card." A third slip was cause for permanent expulsion, although group members might help the unfortunate alcoholic privately.

If you came into A.A. in Little Rock, Arkansas, you were initiated into the program via something called the "Little Rock Plan." Specifically, a newly sober person had to leave his or her job for two weeks, and was required to spend that entire time within the confines of the Little Rock A.A. clubroom, preparing a "case history" and fulfilling other assignments given by a sponsor. If this was successful, he or she would be admitted into the program, but if the new member had a slip, he or she was placed with other backsliders in "the slip squad"—a kind of probation—where they might spend from two weeks to six months before being once again recognized as a full member.

Writing in Grapevine, with the tone of fond exasperation that he so often took in such situations, Bill W. wrote: "If all of these edicts had been in force everywhere at once. . . about nine-tenths of our oldest and best members could never have got by!" Fortunately, most groups in A.A. in the 1940s embraced the Big Book principle that "the only requirement for membership is a desire to stop drinking."

Where It All Begins...

Top row L-R: *Papinachois Roundup, Terrebonne, Quebec* • *The Eye-Opener Group, Naugatuck, CT* • *Keep It Simple Group. Hope Mills, NC*
Center row L-R: *Saturday Night Live Group, Canton, MI* • *New Central Ohio Group* • *The Sierra Fellowship Campout, Shaver Lake, CA*
Bottom row L-R: *The Fifth Tradition Group, Oakville, Ontario* • *441 Group, Margate, FL* • *Church Without Walls Group, Rincón, Puerto Rico*

Top row L-R: No Frills Group, Bellmore, NY • Crossroads Group, Orlando, FL • Midnite Group, New York, NY
Center row L-R: No Matter What Group, Las Vegas, NV • Carry the Message Group, St. Louis, MO • The Wake-Up Group, Mandeville, LA
Bottom row L-R: Sunday Serenity Group, Chaska, MN • Rusinga Island Group, Western Kenya • Singleness of Purpose Group, Winchester, VA

戒酒無名會

PRIZONIER?

contactează
**ALCOOLICII
ANONIMI**

EXISTĂ O
IEȘIRE !

tel:

adresa:

e-mail:

PART THREE

A.A. Around the World

CAPTAIN JACK AND THE LONERS

"I have few contacts ashore with A.A. and have to rely on the Book and 'The Guy Upstairs.' Are there any books or literature to which I can subscribe?"

—CAPTAIN JACK LETTER TO G.S.O., MARCH 1946

The son of a clergyman, Captain Jack S. joined the Merchant Marine during World War I and by the outbreak of World War II was the chief officer of an oil tanker plying the South Pacific. He was also an alcoholic whose disease only worsened when friends died during the hostilities. He was drinking a quart a day when he found an article about A.A. in the January 1946 *Reader's Digest* "and I believed it was what I had been looking for all my life."

The problem was, Jack led a wandering existence, at sea constantly, moving from port to port. How was he to stay sober? He wrote to A.A. Headquarters in New York in March of 1946 explaining that "in my position, I am unable to attend meetings and [I] live day in and day out with people who drink." A staff member provided him with the names of A.A. members in far-flung cities, encouraging him to write to them. Thus was born what Jack called "The Far East Internationalist Group," soon shortened to the Internationalists. It was essentially a round-robin meeting via letter-writing. As Jack said: "Letters started to come in from Australia, from Hong Kong, from Bombay, India: two or three seamen wrote to G.S.O., who in turn sent letters to me."

Jack died at the age of 91 in 1988, with forty-two years sobriety, but by that time the Internationalists had expanded to include so-called "Loners"—those unable to attend meetings regularly because there is no meeting where they live or work. These stayed (and continue to stay) in touch via regular correspondence and by dint of *The Loners-Internationalists Meeting (LIM)*, a confidential bimonthly bulletin. Even more, A.A.'s worldwide growth can in no small part be attributed to Captain Jack and the Internationalists spreading the word around the globe.

SOBER AT SEA ~ *In 1950, the staff of the Grapevine published excerpts from letters written by sailors trying to stay sober while at sea.*

"We usually load in Abadan, Iran, Bahrain Island, Arabia or Palembang, Sumatra. Any of you fellows happen to see this ship, come aboard and look up the Third Assistant Engineer. I will not offer you a drink, but you can ride my bicycle and I guarantee that you will derive more pleasure from that than we ever got out of bending our elbow at the bar." – *From Robert Lee M. on the S.S. Stanvac Hong Kong*

"In Durban . . . I calmly and sanely (that's what I thought) decided 'to hell with it' . . . [and] after nine months I skidded from joint to joint with brassy fluff hanging on my arm and a brainful of alcoholically big ideas. . . ." – *From Bob A. on the S.S. Sideling Hill*

"There's hardly anything to report this time, same run, same fellows; the weather is lousy, no sun for the last five days and off the coast of Mexico heading for California . . . I really missed my meetings last trip but made all I could. I imagine some seagoing fellow wrote, 'Saturday night is the loneliest night in the week.'" – *From John M. on the S.S. Hibuerus*

CANADA: Together in Fellowship

At pivotal times during the course of its history, Alcoholics Anonymous has been indebted to nonalcoholics for their essential support—Dr. William Silkworth; Henrietta Sieberling, who introduced Bill W. to Dr, Bob; Sister Mary Ignatia; and Ruth Hock, Bill's selfless secretary, just to name a few.

Another of these essential nonalcoholics, the Reverend George Little, a 56-year-old Toronto minister, had been trying and failing for years to get alcoholics sober. Early in 1941, he read a newspaper review of the Big Book, ordered a copy and was so impressed that he immediately began mimeographing chapters and passing them around to those whom he thought it would help. One of these was a parishioner of Little's who was having "a little trouble holding his liquor." With the help of the Big Book (and the good Reverend Little), the alcoholic sobered up, and he and Little began helping other Canadian drunks.

The March 1941 Jack Alexander article about A.A. in the *Saturday Evening Post* received wide distribution in Canada, and Little met more alcoholics who asked him about A.A. He continued to order copies of the Big Book and pass them out; he was such an advocate that A.A. Headquarters granted him Canadian distribution rights in 1942. There were as yet no Canadian meetings—although some Windsor, Ontario, A.A.s crossed the river to Detroit to attend meetings there—but that was about to change. On January 13, 1943, Little and a

clergyman friend, the nonalcoholic Reverend Percy Price, joined six alcoholics to hold Canada's very first A.A. meeting in a room above the Little Denmark Tavern in Toronto. A second one was held there a week later, and Canadian A.A. was off and running.

In April 1944, a young Quebec banker named Dave B. reached a horrible alcoholic bottom. Forcibly separated from his wife and young son, committed to a hospital for the insane and classified by the state as a "habitual drunkard," he was considering suicide when he remembered the copy of the Big Book that his sister in Connecticut had sent him. He read the book, called A.A. Headquarters in New York, and spoke with secretary Bobby B., who told him: "We'll help you."

In October, Bobby sent him the names of 400 Canadian alcoholics who had written the New York Office seeking help and Dave B. became what Bill W. would later call a "marathon Twelfth-stepper," tirelessly calling on drunks and even bringing them into his own home, despite the fact that some of them drank his wife's perfume and stole food from the family. Dave B. is considered the father of A.A. in Canada and especially Montreal, the center of French-speaking A.A. Quebecois activity. A.A. meetings were conducted in French there fifteen years before they arrived in France and A.A. lit-

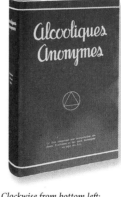

Clockwise from bottom left: The Reverend George Little; Toronto's Little Denmark Tavern; Alcooliques Anonymes, the Quebecois edition of the Big Book.

erature is routinely translated into French. The first French-language Big Book (*Gros Livre* or *Alcooliques Anonymes*) was published in 1963 and the French-Canadian version of the Grapevine, known as *La Vigne*, appears regularly.

By 1949, in an astonishing spurt of growth, the Fellowship had spread across Canada, from Toronto to the Northern Territories, from the Maritime Provinces to British Columbia. Vast distances sometimes separated people from their meetings—and still do—but by car, plane, snowmobile, dogsled and skis, they managed to get there.

Today, there are more than 77,000 A.A. members in Canada, attending more than 4,000 meetings. As a token of the close relationship between A.A. in Canada and A.A. in the United States, one yearly General Service Conference, one board of trustees, and one A.A. General Service Office in New York unite the entire North American Fellowship.

THE WORLD SERVICE MEETINGS

~ The World Service Meeting (WSM) has its roots in Bill W.'s 1950 trip to Europe, where he visited A.A. groups in seven countries that were experiencing the same problems encountered in the U.S. and Canada when A.A. was just getting on its feet — the need for A.A. literature in their own languages; the difficulty of putting together service structures; and the controversies that naturally arose within groups. In the mid-1960s, Bill began thinking of a way to help international groups with these problems.

"As a beginning," Bill wrote the General Service Board in October 1967, "I propose a World Service Meeting—not a *conference*, since it would not be fully representative of world A.A.—to be held in the fall of 1969."

There have now been twenty-three World Service Meetings. Held every two years, alternating between New York and another country, the WSM brings together delegates from A.A. service offices and boards around the globe to talk over common problems and share common solutions to help carry the message of Alcoholics Anonymous wherever it is needed.

The First World Service Meeting, October 1969, New York City.

HOW MANY WAYS CAN YOU SAY "HANGOVER?"

~ A.A. initially spread around the world by word of mouth, but soon thereafter came the printed page for alcoholics hungry to understand the tenets of the program. Early on, Bill W. and others in the Fellowship came to the conclusion that, as Bill later wrote, "a society like ours ought to control and publish its own literature." Today, Alcoholics Anonymous Worldwide Services, Inc. (A.A.W.S.), the publishing arm of A.A.'s General Service Board, preserves the integrity and continuity of literature—the Big Book, the Twelve and Twelve, *Living Sober*, and other essential A.A. texts—helping oversee translations into languages as disparate as the Twi language of Ghana and Rarotongan, the language of the Cook Islands.

A.A. Literature: Many voices, one message.

Often translations arise locally, and then it becomes the job of A.A.W.S. to make sure that they are accurate and consistent. For instance, during the 1960s, '70s, and early '80s, as A.A.'s Spanish-speaking membership grew quickly, a number of translations of the Big Book (*Alcohólicos Anónimos*) undertaken independently in several Spanish-speaking countries were in circulation. But the adaptations frequently disagreed and, moreover, contained numerous regionalisms. Such as the word "hangover": Mexicans spoke of their *cruda*; Colombians, their *guayabo*; Central Americans, their *goma*; and Ecuadorians, their *chuchaque*. A.A.W.S translators finally settled on *resaca*, which also means "undertow."

Translations of the Big Book and other A.A. literature often take years to perfect, but, in the end, it's worth it, since getting it right means saving the lives of alcoholics in countries all over the world.

HELPING ALCOHOLICS AROUND THE GLOBE

The spread of Alcoholics Anonymous around the globe was not a planned decision, but rather the organic growth of a movement whose time had come. Beginning in the early 1940s, however, a number of serendipitous events helped bring A.A. to the attention of the world.

In a review of the Big Book published in the *Houston Press* in April of 1939, the Reverend Harry Emerson Fosdick—a prominent New York clergyman whose brother Raymond ran the Rockefeller Foundation—wrote that "this extraordinary book deserves the careful attention of anyone interested in the problem of alcoholism." As it happened, this was the same review that inspired the Reverend George Little to order a copy of the Big Book and go on to help found A.A. in Canada.

After reading a copy of an article on Alcoholics Anonymous in the *American Journal of Psychiatry*, Dr. Sylvester Minogue, the medical superintendent of Rydalmere Hospital in Sydney, wrote a letter to the journal requesting information on A.A., setting the stage for the startup of A.A. groups in Australia.

Captain Jack S. read a January 1946 article in *Reader's Digest* (condensed from a Grapevine article) entitled "My Return From the Half-World of Alcoholism." The story of an ex-Marine's struggle to overcome his alcoholism, it was this article that led Captain Jack to write A.A. Headquarters in New York, asking for help. And through Captain Jack, seagoing A.A.s, or Internationalists, carried the word to other alcoholics.

Mostly, however, the story of the spread of A.A. around the world is the story of individuals—a soldier, a vacationer, a doctor, a student—seeking sobriety and finding others like them. The extraordinary thing about the spread of A.A. to more than 170 countries—with a worldwide membership of over two million—is that the message of the program transcends cultures, languages, religion and national boundaries. Simply put, alcoholics, in any language, understand other alcoholics.

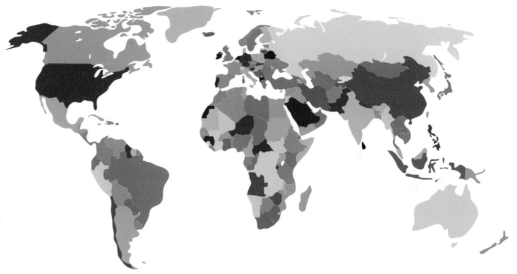

"Outside in the cold Antarctic night the wind may be howling and a blizzard raging. It's not uncommon for the wind chill temperature to drop to minus 80 degrees or lower. Inside though we're warm with our Big Book, coffee pot, and fellowship."

—Kelly J., Ross Island, Antarctica

COUNTRY BY COUNTRY....

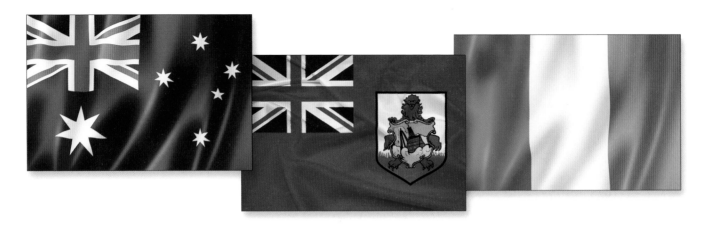

AUSTRALIA

In a letter written in 1945 to Archie McKinnon, a psychiatric nurse interested in helping alcoholics in Sydney, Bobbie B. of A.A. Headquarters provided the names of two other men who shared the same aim: Dr. Sylvester Minogue and Fr. Tom Dunlea, the founder of Boystown in Australia. The three nonalcoholics banded together to form the country's first A.A. group, with Rex A. the first member to achieve and maintain sobriety.

BERMUDA

After seeking advice from A.A. Headquarters, Steve V., an A.A. member formerly of Trenton, New Jersey, formed a group in St. Georges, Bermuda, in 1945. It jumped from two to six members within a month and grew quickly thereafter. The next year, the *Hamilton Mid-Ocean News* published a series of twelve articles on Alcoholics Anonymous.

IRELAND

When Philadelphia A.A. member and former tavern owner Connor F. traveled to Ireland with his wife, he sought alcoholics to bring to sobriety. When they visited a Dublin sanitarium, a doctor introduced them to patient Richard P. of Belfast. After reading the Big Book presented to him by Connor, Richard wrote to a number of contacts who had learned of A.A. through the nonalcoholic Fr. Tom Dunlea, of Australia. Ireland's inaugural A.A. group met in a room at the Country Shop on Dublin's St. Stephen's Green in 1946.

AFGHANISTAN | AMERICAN SAMOA | ANGOLA | ANGUILLA | ANTIGUA AND BARBUDA | ARGENTINA | ARUBA

MEXICO

Americans Lester F. and Pauline D. organized a group for Mexico City's English-speaking community in 1946. Meanwhile, a Mexican resident of Cleveland, Ricardo P., translated portions of the Big Book into Spanish. The importation of Spanish-language alcoholism-related publications and the creation of Spanish-speaking A.A. groups was approved at a late-summer conference of Mexico's Board of Public Information.

SOUTH AFRICA

In 1946, the A.A. movement sprung to life in South Africa in three different places. The founders, unknown to one another, were Arthur S., who read of A.A. in *Reader's Digest*, contacted A.A. Headquarters in New York, and formed a group in Johannesburg; Pat O'F., of Capetown, who also consulted New York; and Val D., who achieved sobriety after reading a copy of the Big Book handed to him by a priest and thereafter started a group in the town of Springs.

NEW ZEALAND

Ian McE., a resident of the South Island town of Richmond, voluntarily admitted himself to a psychiatric hospital in an effort to sober up. There, he came across the *Reader's Digest* article "Maybe I Can Do It Too." Struck by his identification with the article's subject, he wrote to Bobbie B. at A.A. Headquarters. His letter launched a long-term correspondence with (and sponsorship by) Bobbie that led to the 1946 formation of the first New Zealand group.

AUSTRALIA | AUSTRIA | BAHAMAS | BAHRAIN | BANGLADESH | BARBADOS | BELGIUM | BHUTAN | BELARUS

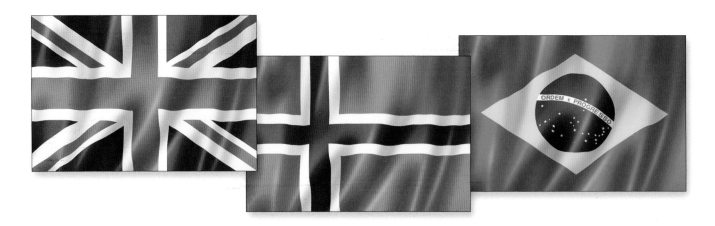

ENGLAND

Though the first official A.A. group in England wouldn't be formed until 1948, the ball got rolling when a traveling American woman, Grace O., wrote to five London alcoholics whose contact information she had gotten from the A.A. Headquarters. Grace scheduled a meeting at the Dorchester Hotel for March 31, 1947. The attendees included Chris S., probably the first person in England to get sober through A.A.; an American with the unlikely name of Flash W; and "Canadian Bob" B., who was instrumental in growing A.A. in England.

NORWAY

George F., a Norwegian immigrant and coffeeshop owner in Connecticut, wrote home after many years to share the good news of his sobriety through A.A. When he learned that his brother, a typesetter for an Oslo newspaper, was an alcoholic one step from ruin, George and his wife sold their shop and moved to Norway. After initially showing no interest in the Twelve Steps, George's brother took the message to heart and got sober almost immediately. Through placing small ads in his paper, George eventually formed a group of A.A. members—Norway's first—in 1947.

BRAZIL

After two years of sporadic correspondence between A.A. Headquarters and a few American residents of Brazil, the New York office listed Herb D. as an A.A. contact. In September 1947, Herb requested and received a batch of A.A. pamphlets and the name of another A.A. member living in Rio de Janeiro. The two men sought members and the first group in Brazil took shape in 1947.

BERMUDA | BOSNIA & HERZEGOVINA | BOTSWANA | BRAZIL | BRITISH VIRGIN ISLANDS | BRUNEI DARUSSALAM

"According to Nepalese culture, alcohol is strictly prohibited in the Brahmin society, and becoming desperate, I returned home. I tried to control my drinking, but gradually all restraint began to fall away ..."

—Puspa D., Kathmandu, Nepal

"My name is Bill, and I'm an alcoholic. I'm also an Aboriginal Australian—a Koori. I got sober...in New South Wales. I was desperate; I was at what the Big Book refers to as 'the jumping off place.'"

—Bill R., West Wyalong, New South Wales, Australia

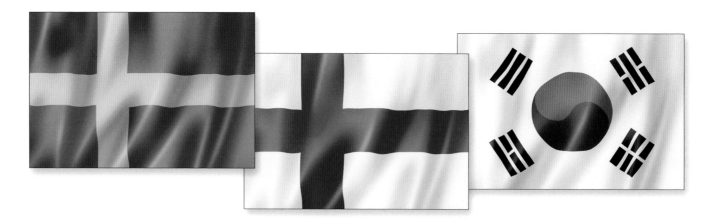

SWEDEN

Frank B., a Swedish-American who got sober in Newark, New Jersey, moved to Sweden and reported to the Newark group that he joined an A.A. group in the town of Borås — much to the surprise of A.A. Headquarters. An exchange of letters between the New York office and the secretary of the Borås group ensued, leading to a listing with A.A. in February 1948.

FINLAND

A few alcoholics joined weekly meetings at the home of a couple employed by the Helsinki Welfare Office. Along with "Mom and Dad," as the leaders were called, they learned of Alcoholics Anonymous when the article "Maybe I Can Do It Too" appeared in the Finnish edition of *Reader's Digest*. In 1948, the group began to adhere to the principles of A.A., as did future Finnish groups.

KOREA

In early 1948, a nonalcoholic priest named Father Mosley started a group in Seoul after he received A.A. literature from New York. Two other groups met sporadically over the next three years, but the first group to be listed with A.A. Headquarters would not be formed until 1952. It was called Yong Dong Po, named after the town in which it first met.

BULGARIA | BURUNDI | CAMBODIA | CAYMAN ISLANDS | CHAD | CHILE | CHINA | COLOMBIA | COOK ISLANDS

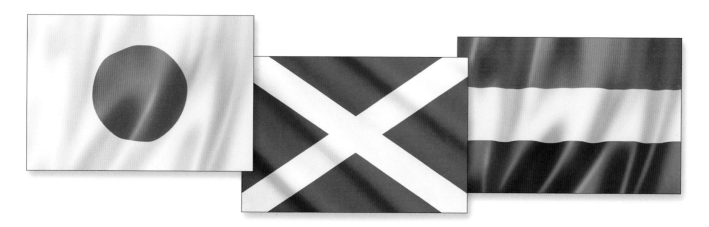

JAPAN

After an article on A.A. appeared in the Pacific *Stars and Stripes*, General Service Headquarters was flooded with letters from American servicemen based in Japan. New York forwarded their names to Harry G., who was in Tokyo writing a book on the War Crime Trials of 1945–48. (Harry had written A.A. Headquarters in December 1947, suggesting that Japan was fertile ground for A.A.) He and an A.A. member from Indiana started an English-speaking group in 1948, eventually leading to the establishment of native groups across Japan.

SCOTLAND

In 1948, Sir Philip D., a Scottish gentleman farmer who had long struggled with alcoholism, traveled to the U.S. at the invitation of the Oxford Group. There he met A.A. member George R., who acquainted him with the Fellowship's principles. Sir Philip returned home determined to stop drinking and to carry the A.A. message. He succeeded and Scotland's first known groups were founded in May 1949 in Edinburgh and in Glasgow.

THE NETHERLANDS

In January 1949, Henk Krauweel, of the Medical Bureau for Alcohol in Amsterdam, reported to General Service Headquarters that he and two of his patients, John V. and Carel A., intended to organize an A.A. meeting in mid-February. They did so, and with much success. In the next two years, a number of groups were started in Rotterdam, Haarlem, the Hague, and other Dutch cities.

COSTA RICA | CUBA | CURAÇAO | CYPRUS | CZECH REPUBLIC | DENMARK | DOMINICA | DOMINICAN REPUBLIC

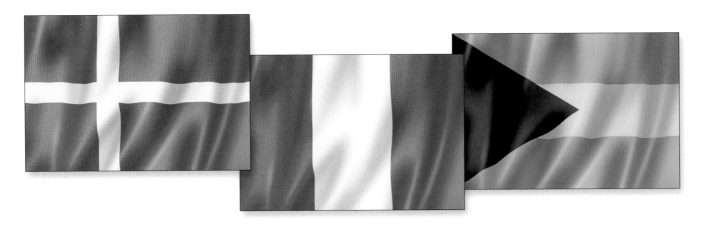

DENMARK

In 1948, a group belonging to a national temperance society called Ring i Ring (meaning "one ring into another") was founded by Dr. Martensen, a doctor who treated alcoholic patients. In the summer of 1949, American A.A. member Gordon McD. and his wife visited Ring i Ring at a meeting place in Lyngby, a small suburb outside Copenhagen. The group changed its name to "Ring i Ring Danish A.A." in January 1950. In the next few years, other Ring i Ring members broke away and held closed meetings based on the Twelve Steps and other A.A. principles.

PERU

After reading in *Look* magazine about ACE (standing for Adverse Childhood Experiences, a treatment for acute alcoholism based on treating childhood trauma), Percy N., an American living in Lima, wrote to the General Service Headquarters asking for its view of the treatment. New York responded by sending him three Alcoholics Anonymous pamphlets. In turn, Percy expressed his wish to become a member and start a group, which he proceeded to do in November 1950.

BAHAMAS

Though there had been inquiries from the Bahamas as early as 1944, Burton L., an A.A. member from Toronto living in Nassau, formed the first stable group in the Bahamas in 1952—four members who met on Sunday afternoons. The group, one of the first in the Caribbean, made a contribution of $6 when it registered with the General Service Headquarters, which had now been renamed the General Service Office (G.S.O.).

ECUADOR | EGYPT | EL SALVADOR | ESTONIA | ETHIOPIA | FAROE ISLANDS | FIJI | FINLAND | FRANCE

GERMANY

A handful of U.S. servicemen, all recovering alcoholics stationed at a U.S. Army base in Munich after the end of World War II, took on the responsibility of forming the first known A.A. group in Germany. They posted notices of a meeting to be held at Hotel Leopold on November 1, 1953. Among the twenty-five attendees were Max, Kurt, and Heindrich, who came together with the Americans in what was to be called Germany's "mother group."

NICARAGUA

In the fall of 1953, Grupo de A.A. La Merced was founded in León by Jack M., who took up residence in Nicaragua in 1950, and then joined A.A. while on a brief visit to the United States. Groups in the capital city of Managua and other Nicaraguan population centers started meeting a decade later, facilitated by G.S.O.

BELGIUM

At a gathering of English-speaking and Belgian alcoholics in Brussels, Jean L. introduced the Big Book and the principles of Alcoholics Anonymous. Within months of the October 1953 meeting, groups started assembling not only in Belgium's capital but also in cities and towns in Flanders and Wallonia.

"In our city of 700,000 people we have a few anonymous alcoholics, but the number of people who can't give up this charming practice is overwhelming .... People come [to meetings], listen, and go back to the delirium of getting drunk. We can only hope that the horse will someday find its way back to the place where it once tasted clear water."

—Valery M., Krasnodar, Russia

"Alcoholics in Sri Lanka deal with the same issues as those in Los Angeles. They work the same Twelve Steps to maintain their spiritual health. A bonus for me is that all four of the country's major religions are represented: Buddhism, Hinduism, Christianity, and Islam."

—D.M., Moratuwa, Sri Lanka

ARGENTINA

In the early 1950s, Hector G. of Buenos Aires was rescued from alcoholism after reading the Big Book and seeking the aid of a physician. He wrote to G.S.O., which sent him A.A. literature in Spanish and asked permission to list him as a contact for referrals. Hector founded Argentina's first known group in 1955.

EL SALVADOR

Edward F., who had carried the Fellowship's message to several alcoholics in Boston and San Francisco, moved to San Salvador with his Salvadoran wife. A friend of his wife introduced Edward to her alcoholic uncle, Don A., and in 1955 the two men formed a group that met at the home of Atilio, a wealthy alcoholic. As membership grew, meetings were moved to the Garcia Flamenco school building. "Mr. Eddie," as he became known, later helped start groups in other Central American countries.

SPAIN

American expatriate Ray C. and fellow alcoholic Dan C. began holding English-language meetings in Madrid in June 1955. By the end of the year membership had increased fourfold and a Spanish-American group began to meet at the sanitarium of Dr. E. Pelaz, a psychiatrist interested in the problem of alcoholism. Before long, the Spaniards formed a separate group, which quickly attracted more members and spurred the formation of A.A. groups countrywide.

GUAM | GUATEMALA | GUYANA | HAITI | HONDURAS | HONG KONG | HUNGARY | ICELAND | INDIA | INDONESIA

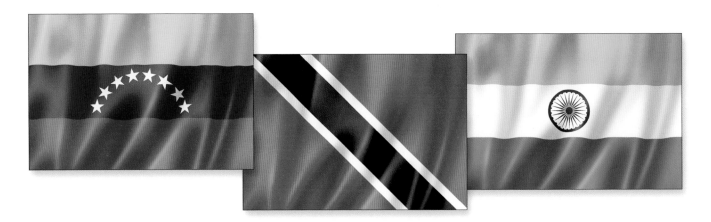

VENEZUELA

A few Americans who gathered for A.A. meetings in Caracas in 1955 placed a small ad in a local English-language newspaper, which drew the attention of Christiaan V., who had previously attempted to start a Spanish-speaking group. With the help of the Americans, Christiaan carried the message to Luis and Clyde, and the three men became the first link in a chain of groups that would spread across Venezuela.

TRINIDAD AND TOBAGO

In March of 1956, G.S.O. in New York received a letter from Stanley M. of Trinidad stating that he was convinced he was an alcoholic and asking to receive information from G.S.O. on how A.A. worked. He was sent literature and advised to get in touch with the only known A.A. member in Trinidad, Reggie G. With the help of a doctor and a clergyman, the two opened the first A.A. meeting in Trinidad in April 1956. Soon A.A. spread to Tobago. As of 2014, this twin island country supports more than 100 groups.

INDIA

In January 1957, Charley M., an A.A. member employed by the National Film Board of Canada on a thirty-six month business sojourn in Asia, contacted Sylvia M. and Supatti M., both New Delhi Loners listed with G.S.O. The three placed an ad in local newspapers, drawing responses from seven alcoholics. By May, New Delhi meetings were attracting eight to twelve people; by year's end, groups would be active in Calcutta and Bombay.

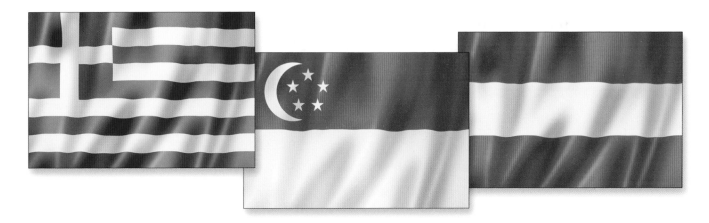

GREECE

An American pilot who was an A.A. member reported to G.S.O. that he had presented a copy of *Twelve Steps and Twelve Traditions* to Rev. Charles Hanna, pastor of the American Church in Athens. Rev. Hanna began corresponding with G.S.O. in early 1957. His efforts brought together three American Loners living in Athens—Frank O. and servicemen Gus and Cal—who held Greece's first A.A. meeting in the port city of Piraeus.

SINGAPORE

Dick D., who regularly corresponded with G.S.O. New York, wrote in March 1958 that the Singapore group, founded in 1957, had twelve members and two likely prospects.

AUSTRIA

In 1959, two A.A. members from Reichenall, Germany, decided to carry the message across the Austrian border to Salzburg. With the aid of their first contact, a physician from a local clinic for nervous diseases, they helped a few alcoholics form a group. To the east in Vienna, two alcoholic women who were being treated in the clinic of a psychiatrist, Dr. Rotter, heard of A.A. and founded a group on their own.

KUWAIT | KYRGYZSTAN | LAOS | LATVIA | LEBANON | LESOTHO | LIBERIA | LITHUANIA | LUXEMBOURG

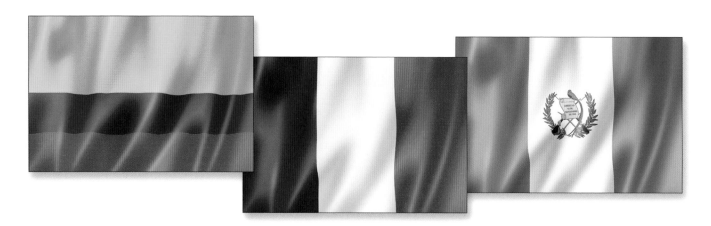

COLOMBIA

After years of failed attempts, a stable Colombian A.A. group was finally formed in January 1959. The principal players were Arturo E. of Medellín and Alejandro S. of Barranquilla, who had met while being treated for alcoholism in a Barranquilla clinic in 1952. While the men twice tried to launch a group, only Arturo was able to stay sober and carry through. His first group, which met in Medellín, planted the seed for those that would follow in Bogotá and other Colombian cities.

FRANCE

While American A.A.s had met in Paris as early as 1949, the first known French-speaking group formed after the newspaper *France Soir* ran a series of articles on Alcoholics Anonymous by journalist Joseph Kessel in the summer of 1960. A letter to the newspaper from Manuel M. (originally from Spain) resulted in his receiving A.A. literature and the start of a group of four: Manuel, François B., Jean M., and Lennard (a Swede).

GUATEMALA

Guatemala's first known A.A. group began meeting in January 1960, through the efforts of Miguel Angel R. and Paulino G. The seed had been planted four years earlier by Reinaldo G., a friend of Miguel's who had joined A.A. in San Francisco before returning home to Guatemala. An Intergroup office would open three years later.

COSTA RICA

Although the Costa Rican government's Committee on Alcoholism (COA), established in 1954, had some success in treating alcoholics, the only connection to A.A. was a perfunctory reading of the Twelve Steps at meetings. After a shaky beginning in 1958, A.A. Grupo Tradicionalista No.I—started by a small group of COA patients—became stable in 1959. By the summer of 1963, eight groups would be meeting countrywide and a General Service Office would open in San José.

The Countries of
THE CARIBBEAN

A.A. groups in the Caribbean, including those in the Bahamas and Trinidad, received support in 1962 when the dedicated Gordon MacD. visited the Antilles and met with secretaries of the groups in the region. The aim of what was called "the Caribbean Crusade," launched by Gordon and other members in 1959, was to develop and reinforce A.A. in the Caribbean and to facilitate cooperation between Caribbean and Latin American groups. Among the islands joining the fold in 1962 were Barbados and Grenada, both in the Lesser Antilles.

THE CHANNEL ISLANDS

Guernsey got on board in 1961 when Pru, a Loner, arranged for meetings to be held in the study of the headmaster of St. Joseph's Roman Catholic School in St. Peter Port. When the group moved to a room above a café, membership grew from six to a dozen. A group started meeting on the nearby island of Jersey in 1962, and small inter-island conventions were held for four or five years—in Guernsey in autumn, in Jersey in spring. The first A.A. group on the Isle of Mann, to the north in the Irish Sea, would be formed in 1966.

MAURITIUS | MEXICO | MICRONESIA | MOLDOVA | MONACO | MONGOLIA | MONTENEGRO | MOROCCO

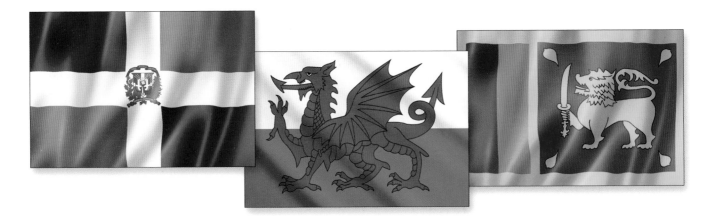

DOMINICAN REPUBLIC

Two A.A. groups began to meet regularly in Santo Domingo in the spring of 1963. One, the Spanish-speaking Grupo Santa Mercedes, grew from two to eighteen members by the end of the year. G.S.O. New York listed as the contact person Abe F., who was also one of two men in the second group, for English speakers; this group, however, would last for only two years.

WALES

The first known group in Wales was founded in Abergavenny in 1963. Until then most alcoholics who wanted to attend A.A. meetings had to cross the border into England. A decade later, the Welsh Borders Intergroup was founded to link groups on both sides of the border. An intergroup has also been established in South Wales—the Cymraig Intergroup, composed of groups in Cardiff, Swansea, Llanelli, and Newport.

SRI LANKA

A Loner in the former Ceylon had been listed with G.S.O. New York since 1959, but not until 1964 was the first known A.A. group in the country formed. Its site was the capital city of Colombo, where a second group took shape a year later. Soon A.A. spread to other Sri Lankan locales. In 1976, a group in the Colombo suburb of Kotahena would mark its third anniversary.

MOZAMBIQUE | MYANMAR | NAMIBIA | NEPAL | NETHERLANDS | NEW ZEALAND | NICARAGUA | NIGERIA

"Finally, I looked up Alcooliques Anonymes in the phone book, found the number and address at the American Church in Paris, and called. It was the first time I admitted that 'alcoolique' was something concerning me."

—ANNIE C.B., PARIS, FRANCE

"I was born nine years ago in Bangkok, Thailand, on the day I found and joined the Fellowship of Alcoholics Anonymous. On that day in June, a drunken habit pattern reached a crossroads and had the opportunity to change to a sober habit pattern."

—ANONYMOUS, BANGKOK, THAILAND

BOLIVIA

An A.A. group in La Paz, Bolivia, was listed with G.S.O. New York in 1965, but little is known of its origins. Better documented were the two men considered A.A.'s Bolivian pioneers: Oscar G. and Jorge L., who met in the city of Santa Cruz in 1971. After three years, Oscar would become a Loner when Jorge left for a job in La Paz. With a local woman named Dorita, Jorge formed an all-new group in La Paz, planting the seed for the eventual start-up of groups in Cochabamba and again in Santa Cruz.

ECUADOR

After a group of physicians from the Ecuadorean city of Cuenca observed A.A. groups in neighboring Colombia, they became instrumental in getting a local group off the ground: Grupo Alianza Amiga, listed with G.S.O. New York in March 1966. The second known group took shape when Eduardo A., who had achieved sobriety through A.A. in Washington, DC, returned home to Guayaquil and arranged with a local priest to hold meetings in his church. In the fall of 1971, the Guayaquil Group helped launch the first known group in the capital city of Quito.

SWITZERLAND

The year 1967 saw the creation of Switzerland's first General Service Office, when the Gremium (German for "committee") began serving German-speaking A.A.s. The country's first known group was French-speaking, however, taking shape in 1956 when an alcoholic in Geneva learned of Alcoholics Anonymous at a lecture, obtained A.A. literature, and arranged a meeting with friends. The first known German-speaking group in Switzerland was launched in 1963 in Lucerne. The first known Italian-speaking group would be formed in the canton of Tessin in 1974.

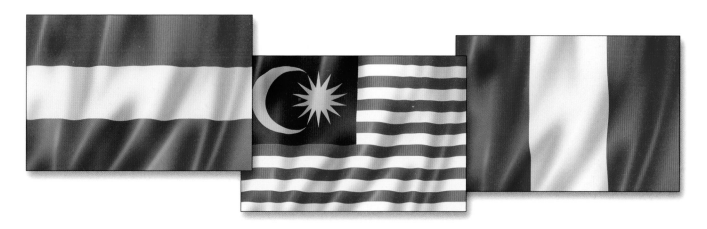

HUNGARY

Midge M., a staff member of G.S.O. New York, traveled to Budapest in June 1969 to attend a conference held by the International Institute on Prevention and Treatment of Alcoholism. While there, she arranged Hungary's first known open A.A. meeting. Members Peter B. of the Netherlands, Inge L. (West Germany), Richard P. (Ireland), and Cecily C. (U.S.) addressed a group of Hungarian alcoholics as Archer Tongue, director of the Institute, translated. While a small group would be formed in Budapest in 1972, A.A. wouldn't become firmly established in Hungary until the late 1980s.

MALAYSIA

In February 1971, Enos C., an A.A. Loner working in Kuala Lumpur, placed a notice in the Malay Mail newspaper seeking other Loners interested in holding meetings. Six weeks later, Enos reported to G.S.O. New York that with the addition of two Canadian A.A.s in Kuala Lumpur, the fledgling Pertama Group already numbered five. By the end of the decade, four more groups started in Sarawak and other Malaysian cities.

ITALY

The start-up of A.A. in Italy was said to be 1972, when a small group of Americans meeting in Rome were joined by locals Giovanni and Ermanno. Assisted by some of the Americans, the two men soon joined with Carol C. to form the first known Italian-speaking A.A. group. Two years later, a group would be founded in Florence, and Milan followed suit in 1976. In 1978, representatives of several groups met to start negotiations with G.S.O. New York for the sponsorship of the publication of *Il Grande Libro* (the Big Book), which was already being translated into Italian. They succeeded, and *Alcolisti Anonimi* was published in 1980.

POLAND | PORTUGAL | QATAR | ROMANIA | RUSSIA | RWANDA | SAINT BARTHÉLEMY | BONAIRE, SAINT EUSTATIUS & SABA

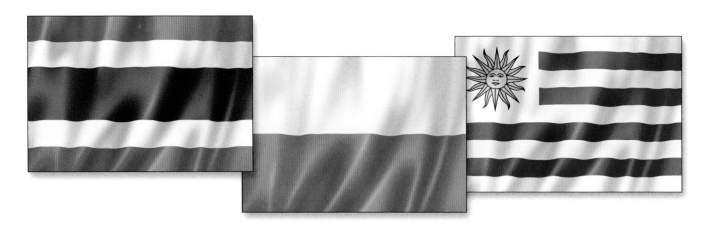

THAILAND

In Bangkok in 1971, two Americans of Irish descent—Jim L., a businessman with three years of sobriety, and Evelyn K., wife of a civil engineer under contract in Bangkok—teamed up to form an A.A. group. The next year they were joined by Jack B., a Redemptorist priest. In 1973, the three moved their meetings from Evelyn's apartment to the Holy Redeemer Rectory and welcomed new member Joanne—the wife of an American Embassy official—and George, a German-born U.S. military member. The stabilization of the Bangkok group soon gave rise to the founding of A.A. groups in Ubon and other Thai cities.

POLAND

A group of alcoholics who had been meeting with physicians and therapists since the mid-1960s in the city of Poznan decided in 1974 to meet on their own and follow the principles of A.A. Led by Rajmund F., a Pole who became sober in 1973 and was fluent enough in English and German to translate A.A. literature, the group took the name Eleusis, after the ancient Greek city the Roman Emperors favored as sanctuary. Growth accelerated, and by June 1985 almost 100 groups would be meeting across the country.

URUGUAY

Pablo L., an actor who underwent detoxification at Montevideo's Clinica del Prado in 1966, was given a copy of the Big Book, and ended up joining the closest A.A. group, which was in Buenos Aires. Returning home, he founded ADEA (for Amigos del Enfermo Alcohólico, or "Friends of the Alcoholic Patient"), where hospitalized alcoholics and their families share experiences. But some aspects of the A.A. program—including anonymity—were rejected. After A.A. Argentina urged ADEA to follow all A.A. Traditions and to take the Fellowship's name, the issue was put to a vote. The ayes had it, and on March 18, 1974, the first known Uruguayan meeting of A.A. was held in Montevideo.

SAINT KITTS & NEVIS | SAINT LUCIA | SAINT MARTIN | SAINT VINCENT & THE GRENADINES | SAUDI ARABIA | SENEGAL

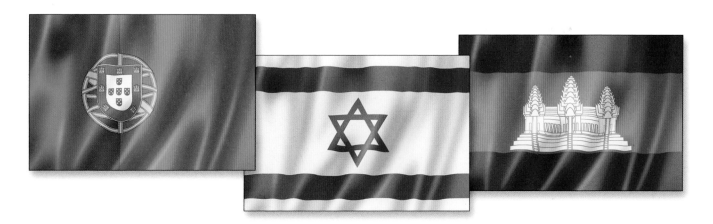

PORTUGAL

English-speaking groups in Portugal had met as early as 1956 in Lisbon and 1959 at Lajes Air Force Base in the nearby Azores. Yet A.A. didn't take root in the country until 1975, when American Ed A. returned from rehabilitation in the United States and began spreading the A.A. message in hospitals. As a result, Portuguese-speaking groups were founded in Lisbon, Oporto, and Algarve. Aiding the growth and stability of the groups was Portuguese-language A.A. literature sent by A.A. Brazil.

ISRAEL

With the aid of Canadian A.A. members who were part of the UN forces in the Middle East, the Shalom Group was formed in Jerusalem in 1975. The next year, member Jay S. reported to G.S.O. New York that twice-weekly A.A. meetings were held in Tel Aviv as well as Jerusalem, in both English and Hebrew. The Shalom Group would also host a two-day convention to celebrate the first anniversary of A.A. in Israel.

CAMBODIA

After the 1975 capture of the Cambodian capital of Phnom Penh by the Khmer Rouge, thousands of Cambodians filled refugee camps along the Thai border. In one camp a U.S. aid worker, whose brother was an A.A. member back in New York, recognized that alcoholism affected many of the refugees, leading her to order and translate A.A. publications. Though up to sixty people attended daily gatherings based on A.A. principles, these meetings ceased when the camp closed. Some fifteen years later, A.A. reappeared in Cambodia when a few members started a group in Phnom Penh.

SERBIA | SEYCHELLES | SINGAPORE | SLOVAKIA | SLOVENIA | SRI LANKA | SOUTH AFRICA | SOUTH KOREA

"*After crossing the harbor, then up a central canal, then across an open stretch of water, I finally dock up. Then comes the trek on foot by flashlight down the muddy path. At this time, our group's name is recalled, if a bit ruefully— 'Camino a la Sobriedad' ('Pathway to Sobriety').*"

—B.C., Islas de la Bahia, Honduras

"*A friend of mine had the 'Great Book' translated into Lithuanian. I read the book and it made me feel more at home in the world .... And so, the first group of A.A. was born in Lithuania. It consisted of three people.*"

—Romas O., Vilnius, Lithuania

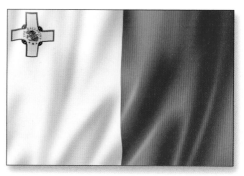

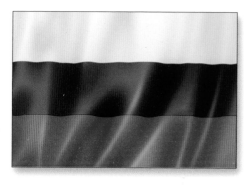

MALTA

In Malta in 1983, the first translations of basic A.A. literature were approved and a Maltese-born member of A.A. Malta attended the biannual European Service Meeting for the first time. Seventeen years prior, in 1966, an Irish veterinary surgeon living in suburban Valletta had listed the Malta Group—originally English-speaking, and later known as the International Group—with G.S.O. New York. In 1981, its Maltese members founded a Maltese Group in the Valleta suburb of Floriana.

LITHUANIA, LATVIA, AND ESTONIA

June 1988 saw the founding of Lithuania's earliest known group, which met in the Vilnius apartment of Romas O., who had become sober when he read a Lithuanian translation of the Big Book in the fall of 1987. In late 1988, Romas and fellow group members visited Riga, Latvia, and began corresponding regularly with that city's first group, founded by Pëteris and Austris in November 1988. In 1989, A.A.s also began meeting in neighboring Estonia, in the town of Tallinn.

RUSSIA

By 1989, three A.A. groups were meeting in Russia—one in Moscow and two in Leningrad. The growth of A.A. in Russia had begun in 1986–1987, through exchange visits between Alcoholics Anonymous members and representatives of Russia's Temperance Promotion Society. Independent groups such as San Francisco's "Creating a Sober World" organization were also instrumental in bringing A.A. to Russia. Growth in Russia proceeded at a rapid pace, expanding to at least 270 groups meeting in more than 100 cities by the beginning of the twenty-first century.

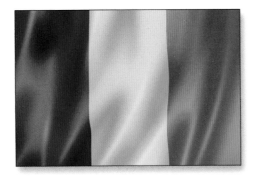

ROMANIA

In 1988, Fran P., an American A.A. teaching English at Romania's University of Timisoara, attempted to start a group with the help of Rodica, an alcoholic student—but the program's reliance on a Higher Power ran afoul of government authorities. Only in 1991, almost two years after the Communist government had fallen, would an A.A. group flourish in Timisoara. In 1993, Petrica and Damian, alcoholics hospitalized in Bucharest, started a group in the capital city with the help of Dr. Doina Constantinescu and Patricia and Lee, an A.A. couple from the United States.

The Countries of SOUTHEAST ASIA

In 1991, around five A.A.s began to meet in Ubud, Indonesia, after which small groups started up in Kuta, Sanur, and Seminyak. The meetings were attended by tourists passing through, but by 2003 some forty Indonesians would join A.A. The early 1990s also saw stable groups of native speakers form in Thailand, Vietnam, Singapore, and Malaysia.

CUBA

In a textbook example of country-to-country sponsorship, Mexico succeeded in getting Cuba's first group going in February 1993: Grupo Sueño (Dream Group), in Havana. The year before, Cubans Ciro V. and Juan A. had asked government officials for permission to provide information about A.A., but without success. Once A.A. Mexico informed the Cuban government of the particulars of A.A.'s program of recovery, the government changed its mind and welcomed the Fellowship.

TRINIDAD AND TOBAGO | TURKEY | TURKS & CAICOS ISLANDS | UGANDA | UKRAINE | UNITED ARAB EMIRATES

CHINA

In August of 2001, two G.S.O. New York staff members and Dr. George Vaillant (nonalcoholic trustee of the A.A. General Service Board) traveled to China to meet with medical practitioners and attend meetings of China's three A.A. groups in existence at the time—two in Beijing and one in Changchun. By invitation, Dr. Vaillant addressed a gathering of some fifty physicians on the subject of alcoholism.

The Countries of
SUB-SAHARAN AFRICA

A.A. France's sponsorship of African countries began with contact between Jean-Yves M. and a Loner from Cameroon, Donatien B., chief warden of a prison and an alcoholic. He achieved sobriety with Jean-Yves's help and became determined to carry the message. Jean-Yves and Jean-François L. traveled to Cameroon in 1997 and were surprised to find that Donatien had started a prison group that grew to fifty-four members. Yearly trips to Africa by A.A. France from 1998 through 2001 facilitated the launching of groups in Benin, Chad, and Togo.

MONGOLIA

The first national convention of A.A. in Mongolia took place in July 2004. It was the result of six years of work. It began when a nonalcoholic physician, Dr. Erdenebager, became interested in A.A. and urged meetings outside of those in treatment facilities in Ulan Bator. Then, in 1999, two newly sober A.A.s and a physician traveled to Moscow to find ways to make A.A. work in Mongolia. When G.S.O. New York received a request from members for literature in the native language, A.A. World Services aided in the publication of the Big Book in Mongolian in 2002.

UNITED KINGDOM | URUGUAY | VANUATU | VENEZUELA | VIRGIN ISLANDS | ZAMBIA | ZIMBABWE

Cleveland, Ohio, July 1950

St. Louis, Missouri, June – July 1955

Long Beach, California, July 1960

Toronto, Ontario, Canada, July 1965

Miami, Florida, July 1970

Denver, Colorado, July 1975

New Orleans, Louisiana, July 1980

Montreal, Quebec, Canada, July 1985

Seattle, Washington, July 1990

San Diego, California, June-July 1995

Minneapolis, Minnesota, June – July 2000

Toronto, Ontario, Canada, June – July 2005

San Antonio, Texas, July 2010

Atlanta, Georgia ✳ July 2-5, 2015

PART FOUR

THE INTERNATIONAL CONVENTIONS
1950 – 2010

The Cleveland Public Auditorium.

The First International Convention
Cleveland, Ohio, July 1950

A.A. marked its fifteenth anniversary with its very first International Convention, with some 3,000 people in attendance at the Cleveland Public Auditorium. There were sessions on A.A. in correctional institutions, A.A. for women, A.A. for young people, A.A. in industry, and the cooperation between A.A. and organized medicine. Significantly, those at this first international event voted to approve the short version of the Twelve Traditions.

At the Big Meeting on Sunday afternoon the only speakers were Dr. Bob and Bill W. Few in the audience knew Dr. Bob was dying of cancer. He spoke for only ten minutes, holding his side in pain. It was the last time Bob spoke to a large A.A. gathering and he used the occasion to remark on the "simplicity of our program" and to say that "our Twelve Steps, when simmered down to the last, resolve themselves in the words 'love' and 'service.'" He died that November.

The Second International Convention
St. Louis, Missouri, June-July 1955

The next Convention was held in St. Louis and became the setting for A.A.'s "coming of age," the occasion when the Fellowship accepted the service structure and the General Service Conference that Bill W. had been promoting.

A press release from the Convention Committee reads: "A dramatic feature of the meeting will occur at Sunday afternoon's closing session when Bill W., the surviving co-founder, will ask the movement to endorse a plan whereby he and other 'elder statesmen' of the society can yield their responsibilities to a representative body which has been functioning under a temporary charter for the past five years." This group, known as the General Service Conference of A.A., now includes ninety-three delegates from A.A. areas in the U.S. and Canada.

In addition, the second edition of the Big Book was launched and Al-Anon, four years old, participated in workshops. The 3,500 attending this Convention were read a telegram from President Eisenhower offering his good wishes.

Top: 5,000 gather at the Second International Convention.
Above: Congratulatory telegram from President Dwight Eisenhower.

The crowd at the Third International Convention in Long Beach, California.

Program and souvenir book from Toronto, A.A.'s first International Convention to be held outside the U.S.

The Fourth International Convention
Toronto, Ontario, Canada, July 1965

At this first Convention held outside the United States, the principal speakers at the Friday and Saturday evening meetings were Bill W., Lois W., and Marty M. The other speakers were nonalcoholic trustee Bernard Smith, and board chairman Dr. John L. Norris. Bill W. spoke both nights, once to tell his story and the other time to review A.A.'s present and future. In all, some 250

The Third International Convention
Long Beach, California, July 1960

The gathering in Long Beach is notable for a couple of reasons, one being that Bill addressed the crowd of about 8,900 for what Nell Wing, his secretary, said was the longest talk he gave—more than two hours. (He also told the memorable story of the evening, during his drinking days, when he arrived home without pants, which is available in the Archives Audio Library). Many notable

figures from the Fellowship's history spoke—not just Bill and his wife Lois, but Sister Ignatia, Marty M., and Dr. Harry Tiebout, a psychiatrist who championed A.A. and brought Marty M. into the program. Showing the spread of A.A. into the wider world, the crowd was entertained by Jane Mansfield, Buster Keaton, Dennis Day, and Peggy Lee—all of whom did so without charge.

members of A.A., Al-Anon, and Alateen, plus twenty-four internationally known nonalcoholic authorities on alcoholism, were featured at sixty-nine sessions.

The theme of the Convention, held at Toronto's Maple Leaf Gardens, was "Responsibility," and Bill and Lois led the more than 10,000 attendees in reciting the Responsibility Declaration at the conclusion of the gathering.

Nearly 20,000 attendees drank half a million cups of coffee at the Sixth International Convention in Denver.

The Fifth International Convention
Miami, Florida, July 1970

 The Fifth International Convention in Miami was to be Bill W.'s last public appearance at an A.A. gathering. Suffering from the emphysema that would take his life the following January, Bill made a surprise appearance at the Sunday morning Big Book meeting before a cheering audience of almost 11,000 attending from fifty states and twenty-seven countries.

These big convention gatherings of Alcoholics Anonymous were beginning to attract the interest of businesses. A letter from a major credit card company to the International Convention organizing committee in April 1970 stated that: "Our worldwide services are of special interest to the members of your organization. We are interested in a manned exhibit at your convention to be held at the Miami Beach Convention Hall." A letter in response from G.S.O. explained that A.A. cannot accommodate any commercial ties to businesses.

The keynote of the Convention was the Declaration of Unity: "This we owe to A.A.'s future: To place our common welfare first; to keep our Fellowship united. For on A.A. unity depend our lives, and the lives of those to come."

The Sixth International Convention
Denver, Colorado, July 1975

Almost 20,000 showed up for this fortieth Anniversary International Convention, far surpassing expectations. Workshops and panel meeting rooms were so crowded that fire department representatives on several occasions stopped more from entering. The Flag Ceremony was held for the first time, with twenty-nine countries represented. It was also the first Convention at which neither Dr. Bob nor Bill was present. To satisfy the huge demand for coffee, the world's largest coffee maker—with servers on both sides of the balcony at the convention hall—was rigged up. It reportedly produced half a million cups daily.

The Seventh International Convention
New Orleans, Louisiana, July 1980

A sort of Mardi Gras parade launched this seventh International Convention, with thirty-three countries participating in the opening Flag Ceremony at the Superdome. More than 22,500 came to the event, celebrating the theme "The Joy of Living." The international aspect of the event was by now firmly established, with simultaneous translation of speakers into French, Spanish, and German. There were two days of workshops and a three-day alkathon (round-the-clock meeting) at the Marriott Hotel. An archives workshop was held for the first time at an International Convention, and the recently completed film *Markings on the Journey* was screened. The son of Dr. Bob addressed the crowd, noting that he was "probably the only person here who was present when Bill met Dr. Bob."

The Eighth International Convention
Montreal, Quebec, Canada, July 1985

Attendance at this fiftieth A.A. Anniversary celebration was 45,000, double the previous turnout for a Convention—and setting a new record for the largest assembly ever for Alcoholics Anonymous. Hotels in Montreal and the surrounding area were so full that some participants stayed seventy-five miles away. Ruth Hock, who as Bill W.'s secretary typed the original manuscript of the Big Book in 1938, was presented with the 5-millionth copy of the Big Book. Among the attendees was Sybil C., one of the first women members in Los Angeles and at the time the longest-sober living woman in A.A.

The Ninth International Convention
Seattle, Washington, July 1990

Seventy-five countries were represented at this International Convention, a number of them formerly parts of the Soviet Union. More than 48,000 attended the gathering, making it at the time the largest convention ever hosted in Seattle. The local host committee made up of Seattle A.A. members numbered 3,000. Nell Wing, Bill's longtime secretary and A.A.'s first archivist, received a commemorative 10-millionth copy of the Big Book. A candle, symbolically lighting the way to sobriety for the still-suffering alcoholic, burned from Thursday night to Sunday morning. The theme of the Convention was "Fifty-five Years—One Day at a Time."

Souvenir book from the 10th International Convention, San Diego.

The Tenth International Convention
San Diego, California, June-July 1995

The theme of the sixtieth Anniversary International Convention—"A.A. Everywhere—Anywhere" was borne out as nearly 56,000 people from the U.S., Canada, and eighty-five other countries gathered in San Diego—making this the biggest A.A. Convention and the biggest convention ever held in San Diego. Among the highlights were an opening night waterfront dance with fireworks exploding across the bay and an opening meeting that saw Jack Murphy (now Qualcomm) Stadium filled to capacity. The Old-Timers Meeting on Saturday night featured 129 members with forty or more years of sobriety, fifteen of whom told their stories.

A band plays at the 11th International Convention in Minneapolis.
Above: Flags of 86 nations.
Top, right: The scene on the convention floor.

The 11th International Convention
Minneapolis, Minnesota, June-July 2000

Fifty years after the first international gathering in Cleveland, 47,500 attendees came to Minneapolis to celebrate the Fellowship of Alcoholics Anonymous. A.A. membership was now about two million worldwide and the Big Book was available in forty languages. The theme was "Pass It On—Into the Twenty-first Century." One memorable event was Walk-the-Walk, in which a stream of attendees from eighty-six nations walked the blue line laid down from the Convention Center to the Hubert H. Humphrey Metrodome on their way to the opening ceremony. The twenty-millionth Big Book was presented to Al-Anon Family Groups in a special ceremony.

2005 International A.A. Convention Toronto

A.A. returns to Canada 44,000 members strong.

The 12th International Convention
Toronto, Ontario, Canada, June-July 2005

Over 44,000 A.A. members congregated in Toronto for the 2005 International Convention to celebrate the seventy years that have brought A.A. from a bond between two sober alcoholics to a worldwide Fellowship. The theme was "I Am Responsible," reprising the theme of the 1965 International Convention, also held in Toronto, where A.A.'s popular "Responsibility Declaration" was first devised.

The 13th International Convention
San Antonio, Texas, July 2010

More than 53,000 A.A. members and guests from around the world celebrated A.A.'s seventy-fifth year in San Antonio, Texas, with the theme "A Vision for You." This was the largest group San Antonio, a frequent convention city, had ever seen. More than 212 meetings and workshops took place at the Convention Center and at several hotels. Meetings were available in French, Spanish, Italian, German, Japanese, Russian, Portuguese, Polish and Swedish. The Marathon Meeting, in English and Spanish, began at midnight Thursday and ran until 7:00 a.m. Sunday.

A.A.'s took in the sights at the 13th International Convention in San Antonio.

The Twelve Steps of Alcoholics Anonymous

1. We admitted we were powerless over alcohol—that our lives had become unmanageable.

2. Came to believe that a Power greater than ourselves could restore us to sanity.

3. Made a decision to turn our will and our lives over to the care of God *as we understood Him.*

4. Made a searching and fearless moral inventory of ourselves.

5. Admitted to God, to ourselves, and to another human being the exact nature of our wrongs.

6. Were entirely ready to have God remove all these defects of character.

7. Humbly asked Him to remove our shortcomings.

8. Made a list of all persons we had harmed, and became willing to make amends to them all.

9. Made direct amends to such people wherever possible, except when to do so would injure them or others.

10. Continued to take personal inventory and when we were wrong promptly admitted it.

11. Sought through prayer and meditation to improve our conscious contact with God, *as we understood Him,* praying only for knowledge of His will for us and the power to carry that out.

12. Having had a spiritual awakening as the result of these steps, we tried to carry this message to alcoholics, and to practice these principles in all our affairs.

The Twelve Traditions of Alcoholics Anonymous

1. Our common welfare should come first; personal recovery depends upon A.A. unity.

2. For our group purpose there is but one ultimate authority—a loving God as He may express Himself in our group conscience. Our leaders are but trusted servants; they do not govern.

3. The only requirement for A.A. membership is a desire to stop drinking.

4. Each group should be autonomous except in matters affecting other groups or A.A. as a whole.

5. Each group has but one primary purpose—to carry its message to the alcoholic who still suffers.

6. An A.A. group ought never endorse, finance, or lend the A.A. name to any related facility or outside enterprise, lest problems of money, property, and prestige divert us from our primary purpose.

7. Every A.A. group ought to be fully self-supporting, declining outside contributions.

8. Alcoholics Anonymous should remain forever nonprofessional, but our service centers may employ special workers.

9. A.A., as such, ought never be organized; but we may create service boards or committees directly responsible to those they serve.

10. Alcoholics Anonymous has no opinion on outside issues; hence the A.A. name ought never be drawn into public controversy.

11. Our public relations policy is based on attraction rather than promotion; we need always maintain personal anonymity at the level of press, radio, and films.

12. Anonymity is the spiritual foundation of all our Traditions, ever reminding us to place principles before personalities.

The Twelve Concepts for World Service

The Twelve Concepts for World Service were written by A.A.'s co-founder Bill W., and were adopted by the General Service Conference of Alcoholics Anonymous in 1962. The Concepts are an interpretation of A.A.'s world service structure as it emerged through A.A.'s early history and experience. The short form of the Concepts reads:

I Final responsibility and ultimate authority for A.A. world services should always reside in the collective conscience of our whole Fellowship.

II The General Service Conference of A.A. has become, for nearly every practical purpose, the active voice and the effective conscience of our whole Society in its world affairs.

III To insure effective leadership, we should endow each element of A.A.—the Conference, the General Service Board and its service corporations, staffs, committees, and executives—with a traditional "Right of Decision."

IV At all responsible levels, we ought to maintain a traditional "Right of Participation," allowing a voting representation in reasonable proportion to the responsibility that each must discharge.

V Throughout our structure, a traditional "Right of Appeal" ought to prevail, so that minority opinion will be heard and personal grievances receive careful consideration.

VI The Conference recognizes that the chief initiative and active responsibility in most world service matters should be exercised by the trustee members of the Conference acting as the General Service Board.

VII The Charter and Bylaws of the General Service Board are legal instruments, empowering the trustees to manage and conduct world service affairs. The Conference Charter is not a legal document; it relies upon tradition and the A.A. purse for final effectiveness.

VIII The trustees are the principal planners and administrators of overall policy and finance. They have custodial oversight of the separately incorporated and constantly active services, exercising this through their ability to elect all the directors of these entities.

IX Good service leadership at all levels is indispensable for our future functioning and safety. Primary world service leadership, once exercised by the founders, must necessarily be assumed by the trustees.

X Every service responsibility should be matched by an equal service authority, with the scope of such authority well defined.

XI The trustees should always have the best possible committees, corporate service directors, executives, staffs, and consultants. Composition, qualifications, induction procedures, and rights and duties will always be matters of serious concern.

XII The Conference shall observe the spirit of A.A. tradition, taking care that it never becomes the seat of perilous wealth or power; that sufficient operating funds and reserve be its prudent financial principle; that it place none of its members in a position of unqualified authority over others; that it reach all important decisions by discussion, vote, and, whenever possible, substantial unanimity; that its actions never be personally punitive nor an incitement to public controversy; that it never perform acts of government; that, like the Society it serves, it will always remain democratic in thought and action.

INDIVIDUAL SUBSCRIPTION $1 A YEAR

AA EXCHANGE BULLETIN

August-September 1965

NEWS AND NOTES FROM THE GENERAL SERVICE OFFICE OF A.A.

305 East 45th Street, New York 17 • Mail address: Box 459, Grand Central Station, New York 17

Vol. 10 No. 4

'I AM RESPONSIBLE'

Greetings To A.A.'s

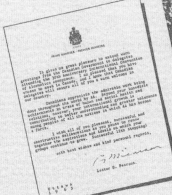

TORONTO, ONT., JULY 4, 1965. —A mighty message of hope for the world's suffering victims of alcoholism thundered forth from here at 10:25 p.m. last night, Saturday, July 3.

The largest assemblage in history of recovered, once-thought-hopeless drunks...more than 10,000 A.A. members, their families and friends representing 30 countries... at that instant solemnly clasped hands and led by Bill W. and Lois, clearly and loudly pronounced this promise of hope in one tremendous, strong voice.

I am responsible. When anyone, anywhere reaches out for help, I want the hand of A.A. always to be there. And for that: I am responsible.

It was the moving climax to the biggest A.A. gathering yet, the 30th Anniversary Year International Convention which brought together A.A., Al-Anon and Alateen members from all over the globe for three days

packed with opportunity to share experiences, strengths, hopes and fun.

In Toronto's vast Maple Leaf Gardens on Friday night a crowd mindful of its own size heard from their own lips the stories of Bill W., A.A.'s co-founder and author of the basic books; Lois W., his wife, the First Lady of the Al-Anon Family Groups; and Marty M., one of A.A.'s first women members.

On Saturday evening an even larger throng heard Bill and nonalcoholic Trustee Bernard Smith, describe one of the most glorious fruits of A.A. recovery from alcoholism; individual freedom to accept responsibility for ourselves and for our share in A.A. as a whole.

"Newcomers are approaching A.A. at the rate of tens of thousands yearly," Bill declared. "Let us not pressure anyone with our individual or collective views. Let us instead accord each other the respect and love due to every human being.

"I trust we shall continue to have tremendous awareness of our responsibilities for improvement," Bill continued.

Attorney Smith, associated with A.A.'s General Service Board for 21 years, said, "You have something great and awesome going for you, treat it tenderly, respect what it has done for you and what it can do for others...

(continued on page 2)

The A.A. Exchange Bulletin for August-September 1965, reporting on the "mighty message of hope" from the Toronto International Convention during that 30th anniversary year.

1935 ❉ *30th Anniversary Year* ❉ 1965

I am responsible...

When anyone, anywhere,
reaches out for help,
I want the hand of A.A. always to be there.
And for that: I am responsible.

Je suis responsable...

Juqondene Nami

Io sono responsabile...

Eu sou responsável...

나는 책임이 있읍나다...

Ik ben verantwoordelijk,

Jeg er ansvarlig

Ég er ábyrgur...

ابا مسؤول...

Oku ou fatangia'aki

ลันรู้จักรัยพิดชอย …

Saya bertanggung jawab…

JESTEM ODPOWIEDZIALNY

JEG ER ANSVARLIG…

Yo soy responsable…   Minulla on vastuu

Ich bin verantwortlich…

…אני אחראי

Ben sorumluyum…

Ke na le maikarabelo…   I am responsible…